1973

AYS

OXFORD MODERN LANGUAGES
AND LITERATURE MONOGRAPHS

THE
POETIC MODES OF
OCTAVIO PAZ

BY

RACHEL PHILLIPS

OXFORD UNIVERSITY PRESS

1972

Oxford University Press, Ely House, London W. 1

GLASGOW NEW YORK TORONTO MELBOURNE WELLINGTON
CAPE TOWN IBADAN NAIROBI DAR ES SALAAM LUSAKA ADDIS ABABA
DELHI BOMBAY CALCUTTA MADRAS KARACHI LAHORE DACCA
KUALA LUMPUR SINGAPORE HONG KONG TOKYO

PRINTED IN GREAT BRITAIN
AT THE UNIVERSITY PRESS, OXFORD
BY VIVIAN RIDLER
PRINTER TO THE UNIVERSITY

TO
EVE, GUY, CLAIRE
AND GRACE
WHOM I LOVE

ACKNOWLEDGEMENTS

I AM grateful for the help of my teachers at the University of Kentucky, especially Dr. Daniel Reedy, and for the encouragement and advice of Dr. Cyril A. Jones, of Oxford University, former tutor and constant friend.

Quotations from *Libertad bajo palabra* are reproduced by permission of the Fondo de Cultura Económica, Mexico. Quotations from *Salamandra* and *Ladera Este* are reproduced by permission of the Editorial Joaquín Mortiz, Mexico.

CONTENTS

ABBREVIATIONS

L.E. *Ladera Este* (Mexico, 1969)
Lib. *Libertad bajo palabra* (2nd ed., Mexico, 1968)
Sal. *Salamanrda* (Mexico, 1962; 2nd ed., 1969)

INTRODUCTION

THE Mexican poet, Octavio Paz (b. 1914), is undoubtedly one of the giants of today's literary world, and the startling diversity of his production in prose and poetry makes any generalization suspect. As a poet Paz is at once his country's most faithful lover and most stringent critic; yet he has had dealings with the Surrealists and his reputation has far surpassed national boundaries. He has absorbed the ancient myths of Mexico and shown an amazing understanding of the Oriental mind, so that the scope of his poetry over the last thirty-five years is phenomenal. The reality which this poetry projects is firmly based on personal responses to the universe, yet it is revealed in a fascinating variety of ways. The crux for Paz lies in the function of poetry as a link between the inner reality of his intuitions and the outer world of which he is a part.

As for his prose works, more immediately relevant to poetry are the aesthetic writings, especially *El arco y la lira* (Mexico, 1967) and certain parts of *Corriente alterna* (Mexico, 1967). At one remove lie his critical writings, both of the visual arts—the works of Marcel Duchamp and Rufino Tamayo,[1] for instance—and of literature, as in the four studies in *Cuadrivio* (Mexico, 1969) on Darío, Lopez Velarde, Pessoa, and Cernuda. *Corriente alterna* has a scope wide enough to include thoughts on a variety of contemporary issues, while *Claude Lévi-Strauss o el nuevo festín de Esopo* (Mexico, 1967) is in large part responsible for the understanding of structuralism in the Spanish-speaking world. An even more recent work, *Conjunciones y disyunciones* (Mexico, 1969), extends to the regions of metapsychology and embraces Eastern and Western trends of thought. Perhaps the best-known prose work is *El laberinto de la soledad* (Mexico, 1959), an analysis of Mexican characteristics written in accordance with what might be called poetic sociology. This has now been brought up to date with the publication of his latest work, *Posdata* (Mexico, 1970).

The various shorter volumes of Octavio Paz's poetry have been published in three major collections. Poems from 1935 to 1957 appear in *Libertad bajo palabra* which has had two editions, in 1960 and 1968. Considerable differences exist between these versions, the latter containing fewer poems, some of these shortened or revised, and the whole rearranged according to a more chronological sequence. In deference to the poet's obvious wishes, all quotations in this study are from the second edition. The *chef-d'œuvre* 'Piedra de sol' is the last poem in both editions of *Libertad bajo palabra*. *Salamandra* contains poems dating from 1958 to 1961, and has also had two editions, the first in 1962, the second in 1969. Though the second edition is 'corregida', no dramatic revision has occurred here. The most recent volume is *Ladera Este* (Mexico, 1969), which includes the shorter collection of the same name, *Hacia el comienzo*, and the very impressive 'Blanco', which appeared separately in a limited, boxed edition in 1967.

Apart from these great volumes, Paz has published two experimental works, *Topoemas* and *Discos visuales*, both of which appeared in Mexico in 1968. The former is a volume of six concrete poems very individualistic in style, and the latter might be described as multi-media communication. Both have been drawn into the scope of this study. No mention has ever been made, however, of the collective poem written in Spanish, French, English, and Italian by Paz in collaboration with the poets Jacques Roubaud, Charles Tomlinson, and Edoardo Sanguineti respectively. This most recent work was published in 1971 by Éditions Gallimard and by Grove Press in an English translation.

The aim of the present study is modest in comparison with Paz's formidable intellect and production, and arrogant in the face of his poetic stature. I have tried to perceive and communicate something of the poetic world which Paz's vision has created. There is no attempt to extract or interpret a message, merely to clarify the linguistic system which is this vision itself. Thus I have referred at length to the texts of poems written throughout Paz's career when these seemed to help to clarify the constant centre from which his ever-evolving poetry grows.

Music provides a convenient analogy to make accessible the basic structure unifying each of Paz's poems individually and his *œuvre* as a whole. Music is the art-form which accepts structure as form itself, and the musical mind *par excellence* is aware of the relationship of parts to each other and of these parts to the whole; therefore, in order to explore the counterpoint between the changing façade of Paz's poetry and the constant pattern behind it, I have used the musical term 'mode' in its strictest sense. This implies an unchanging relationship of sounds to each other within each mode, and a changing effect on the ear which receives the sound of the different modes themselves. The Greeks evolved as a frame for their music several systems, each of which is evocative of a certain atmosphere or mood. The internal arrangements of these systems were prescribed according to patterns which created the difference between, for instance, the Dorian and the Lydian modes. Thus the relationship of notes to each other within each mode is a given factor, but the mood created by each mode differs according to the active or passive functions of notes within each individual system. In effect the tensions set up by the differing relationships of notes create the varying moods of each individual mode. Thus a mode is at once a closed system and a flexible tool in the hands of a musician, and modes stand to each other in a relation of kinship (they are all variations on the possible combinations of tones and half-tones), but are distinguished by their individual flavour.[2] In the same way, behind Paz's poems lies the constant relationship of the poet both to reality and to his creation, though the surface aspects are multiple and diverse.

To establish the existence of a basic structure and to decide upon a modal approach to Paz's poetry are the first and easiest steps. The definition of the modes themselves is less simple because of the variety of criteria and terminology to which this system leaves itself open—at once its virtue and its challenge. Yet it seems possible, without in any way violating the flexibility of the poet's expression, to proceed in a series of concentric circles, Pythagorean spheres, as it were, from the outer circumference inwards. At any rate one can establish a progression from the mode which depends most upon external referents and thematic content, to the most distilled expression of this same underlying vision.

The paradigm behind the poetic modes, like the sequence of whole tones and half-tones fundamental to each musical mode, is that of transcendence through suffering. This is the rebirth following death in myths; it is the integration of the personality after exploration of the subconcious by surrealism; the boundaries of the self are enlarged in erotic love; the emergence of a work of art follows the struggle of the artist with experience and medium. And since 'transcendence' is a term which will recur in this study, given the premise on which it is based, initial clarification is

necessary. Paz writes as a visionary poet and his later poetry rises
to a level where distinctions between creative and religious experiences are hard to draw, so that this matter becomes crucial in
approaching what Amado Alonso calls the expressive system
('sistema expresivo')[3] of this poet.

It is clear that within the frame of reference of Paz's poetry the
'transcendent experience' felt by the poet and shared with the
reader is open to discussion only on the aesthetic level. If the
aesthetic transcendence is fused at times with what may be called
truly a mystical self-transcending which raises it beyond the self-
awareness of the subject, then the experience enters a realm where
the literary critic may not follow. Thomas Merton has written
perceptively on the transcendent experience in an essay by this
name,[4] and his basic point is that which Paz himself makes in his
comments on the concept of *sunyata* (the void) within the framework of Mahayana Buddhism (*Ladera Este* 179–82 and 'Comentario' to *Topoemas*). The attainment of perfect wisdom—mystic
union for the Christian, Prajnaparamita for the Buddhist—implies
so revolutionary a change in the subject that there can no longer
be said to be a subject or an experience. Identity by definition is
transcended—it has gone beyond itself and is merged with the
Divine Being, the object of its quest. If the empirical ego is aware
of itself as having been transcended, then this experience has not
taken place. Hence the paradoxes of the Hindu Sutras and the Zen
koans, the injunction 'If you encounter the Buddha, kill him',[5] or
Meister Eckart's words, 'We love God with His own love; awareness of it deifies us.'[6] Mystic transcendence involves an ontological
experience of what Merton calls 'superconsciousness', literally a
being raised above oneself. In Buddhism the individual ego 'finds
itself to be in reality the enlightened Buddha mind'. The Christian
'enters into the self-emptying (crucifixion) and glorification
(resurrection and ascension) of Christ'.[7] In both cases the path lies
through 'self-emptying' of the empirical ego in the Ground of
Being.

In the context of literary criticism this truly 'transcendent'
experience is irrelevant and dicussion of it irreverent. It must be
understood that there are fundamental differences between the
self-fulfilling 'rite of passage' from one level of awareness to a
higher one in erotic or aesthetic terms and the mystical transcendence described above. The question is important, as Paz

himself wanders into metaphysical realms in his recent poems. I limit myself, therefore, to a secular use of the term 'transcendent experience' in connection with Paz's poems. I do not exclude an extension of the term to its rightful (mystical) level, nor do I imply it.

This study claims, therefore, only a limited scope, namely to isolate by an examination of his poetry the structure upon which Octavio Paz's work rests. Certain 'poetic modes' have suggested themselves, and within these a simple method of textual exegesis has been used, in the hope of revealing the constant heart of the poet's writings. In examining the relationship of the parts of a poem to each other and to the whole which is the poem itself, in the same way considering the relationship of one poem to another as parts of Paz's poetic world, I have tried to keep in harmony the two symbiotic components of every literary work, defined by C. S. Lewis as *Logos* and *Poiema*.[8] For the poem both 'means' and 'is'. In trying to search out the structure fundamental to Paz's poetry and distinctively his own, I have tried to allow that which is said (*logos*) to speak through yet not obscure the creation which he has made (*poiema*).

I

THE MYTHIC MODE

ONE of the most ironic paradoxes of modern man is that, having by the use of reason desacramentalized his world, he finds himself engaged in a constant search for a pivotal meaning to life. The eighteenth century tried in various ways to replace Christian teleology by the apotheosis of rationalism and the idea of progress, while the twentieth century tries to place human concern at the centre of our view of existence. Yet neither has succeeded in reproducing the firmness and conviction which surrounded the ideology of the Christian tradition and the myths of the so-called primitive societies. In these societies life is 'real' only to the degree that it is sacramental, that is, imitative of the original patterns of creation and order which brought existence from eternity. Primitive tribes have no awareness of historicity; they live according to a cyclical view of the cosmos, and all their acts, even the simplest, such as building a house, are imitations of the first act of creation, and meaningful to them only by virtue of that imitation.[1] Thus living is a daily sacrament, a constant return to the moment before time, and a reminder of the eternal truths of the tribe. Christianity took from the Judaic-Hebrew religion the element of faith, but its view of life is also sacramental, since each soul can re-enact the passion, death, and resurrection of Jesus Christ. While Christian, or actually Catholic, beliefs held sway over men's minds, the prevailing world-view was solidly based in the revealed truths of Christianity which, like the cosmic mythologies, kept men in touch with the eternal, or at least aware of how, through the sacrament, time might be transcended.

With the gradual loosening of the hold of religion on men's minds, the position of the poet altered. Milton still stood in a universe organized according to the age-old patterns. But by the nineteenth century the poet had taken over much of the role formerly held by the priest in society; as the old mysteries lost in pertinency, their spokesmen became less relevant to men's lives.

Literature assumed a much more transcendental place in society with the Romantics—witness Novalis and his blue flower, or Victor Hugo and his mission as prophet. And for Wordsworth the imagination became the faculty which transmits mystic insight to the mind.

Thus the modern poet is a Janus figure. Looking within himself he finds the disorientation of all our lives, the lack of a given and acceptable pattern of beliefs. He may find his pattern—certainly his search is that of Everyman, and in his search lies his relevance. Looking outward he sees a society which has cast off its beliefs and lost its myths, and which turns to art for a re-creation of the archetypal forms which primitive man in one way, Christian man in another, relied upon to live. The re-creation of myth, whether directly or indirectly, is what gives universal meaning to the greatest modern works of art, from Joyce's *Ulysses* to Schoenberg's *Jacob's Ladder*, or Octavio Paz's 'Piedra de sol'.

The greatness of Paz's poetry seems to lie in its direct confrontation of the human condition, and in its expression of the evolving consciousness of the poet as he searches for his own answers and his own break-throughs. The impression which Paz's total *œuvre* conveys is that of a man in search of a myth, that is, a pattern of beliefs by which time-bound existence may be eternalized and made 'real'. With no traditional faith to fall back on, Paz has to use whatever is at his disposal. Thus he turns to the paradigms or traditional mythologies as vehicles for his own spiritual progress, drawing from them the symbolic meanings which create the structure of myths[2] and which reappear in different forms in every manifestation of the human thirst for transcendence. Among those poems of his which rely on the structure of mythologies, there are those concerned with the symbolism of the Nahua religion, others which draw on traditional Graeco-Roman archetypes, and yet others in which the mythologies of India, Brahmanism, Buddhism, and Tantra provide the key to their symbolic meanings. Since these divisions have roughly a chronological sequence, it will be appropriate to deal with them in this order, as the changes in the poet's style will thus correspond to a change in thematic material.

MEXICAN MYTHS

The importance of Mexico in Paz's work cannot be overestimated.[3] The foreigner feels love of country and concern for it in all Paz's work, somctimes directly, sometimes between the lines, sometimes expressed with bitterness, often with nostalgia. The Mexican recognizes this identification of self with fatherland and appreciates it most completely, as Carlos Fuentes showed in a *Mundo Nuevo* interview[4] in which he paid tribute to Paz as having become more Mexican through exile. Fuentes went further, in fact, and attributed much of Paz's creative inspiration to his 'gran arraigo espiritual' to Mexico. Mexico is felt in Paz's poetry in many ways: it is a place in Nature with its beauties and its horrors, a tradition rich in myths and spiritual lessons, and an autocracy to be mourned. Paz does not regard himself as a political writer, but issues of humanitarianism and personal freedom continually stir him, and his relationship with his country has much of a love–hate dichotomy. Along with pride in rediscovering the religious glories of the Nahua myths, a burning thread of indignation at the injustices which dehumanize man runs through all his poetry, in the 1937 poem 'Entre la piedra y la flor' (*Libertad bajo palabra* 80–7) and the much later 'Intermitencias del Oeste (3)' (*Ladera Este* 68–9)[5] alike.

'Entre la piedra y la flor' is not a poem which deals directly with the mythology of Mexico, yet it cannot be ignored when Paz is being considered against the background of his country and its tradition. The poem is a bitter indictment of the exploitation of one human being for another's gain, and the Mexican peasant in it stands isolated between the rocky ground which he has inherited and the symbolic loneliness of the henequen flower. 'Entre la piedra y la flor' was written in Yucatan while Paz was working on a social project among the peasants, namely, the founding of a secondary school for workers' children. It has five segments, and is based on an irregular combination of eleven- and seven-syllabled lines; but the poet varies his metre at will, lengthening the line, for instance, to convey the interminable weariness of

> Fiebre y jadeo de lentas horas áridas,
> miserables raíces atadas a las piedras.
> (*Lib.* 80)

The poem is introduced by a couplet from Quevedo, 'Nada me desengaña / El mundo me ha hechizado', and the opening creates a landscape lying as though bewitched under the burning sunlight. The first couplet speaks of an environment not only hostile but deadly to man:

> En el alba de callados venenos
> amanecemos serpientes.
> (*Lib.* 80)

It is a land of rocks, of thirst, and of light as sharp as steel, and the henequen plant looms over all as the incarnation of the rage and helpless fury which is man's response to such surroundings:

> Bajo esta luz de llanto congelado
> el henequén, inmóvil y rabioso,
> en sus índices verdes
> hace visible lo que nos remueve,
> el callado furor que nos devora.
> (*Lib.* 80)

Death is ever-present in this landscape, where light breaks against itself, having annihilated all else. Water is heard only in dreams, or felt as a subterranean presence imprisoned in a tomb of rock. Even the birds which fly up at six in the evening are silent, 'pájaros mudos, barro alado', and the clouds in the sky are cruel, clawing their way across the heavens. There is a night-time truce when water is heard as a moan, and when man turns from death to dreams, but the henequen stands sentinel:

> Es la venganza de la tierra
> la mano de los hombres contra el cielo
> (*Lib.* 82)

In the second section (*Lib.* 82–3) the poet in bewilderment questions the land he finds himself in, and answers his own questions. This is a land born before death itself, where dreams are replaced by thirst. Here the earth can give only one plant, the 'flor funesta, / su espada vegetal', the henequen, which seems to come from blind cellars, 'duras capas de olvido donde el tiempo no existe'. The plant grows in a bitterness of concentration until, after a quarter of a century, its one flower blooms, 'isla inmóvil, / petrificada espuma silenciosa'. So much silent struggle, so much suffering '¿... surge en tu llama rígida, desnuda, / para cantar, sólo, tu muerte?'

In this land without consolation, without myths, there is still a living proof of transcendence—man. Section three opens as a song

of triumph to man, undefeated by thirst and barrenness, symbol of
life in the middle of the desert—'húmedo y persistente como lluvia
. . . como un árbol hermoso y ultrajado . . . como un río entre las
llamas / como un pájaro semejante a un relámpago'. Existence is
its own triumph, and man survives 'entre la piedra y la flor', held
by 'un pulso aéreo', between the blazing heat of the sun and the
menacing agave. Man lives his physical existence, but he lives on
another level too, that of dreams, while in an Unamunesque, or
Borgian paradox, he is also dreamt:

> Alguien te sueña, solo,
> Tu nombre, polvo, piedra,
> en el polvo sediento precipita su ruina.
>
> (*Lib.* 84)

Then the tyranny of materialism obtrudes, and the fourth
section bursts into bitter irony as the timelessness of man in his
environment is compromised by the economy which chains him
and controls his very innocence:

> Ángel de tierra y sueño,
> agua remota que se ignora,
> oh condenado,
> oh inocente,
> oh bestia pura entre las horas del dinero . . .
>
> (*Lib.* 85)

In the last section the poet turns to the henequen, to join his angry,
helpless rebellion to the mute fury of the plant—two witnesses to
oppression and misery:

> Dame, llama invisible, espada fría
> tu persistente cólera,
> para acabar con todo . . .
>
> (*Lib.* 86)

The plight of one becomes that of all, and the burning flame of the
plant is man's voice against his own solitude, and against time,
along whose road we are led to death.

'Entre la piedra y la flor' offers no gods to save man; no reference
higher than man himself is hinted at. In 'El cántaro roto' from
La estación violenta, (*Lib.* 232–6), the old faiths are seen as
'broken pitchers' no longer sufficient to regenerate the spirit of man
in a world still seen as unjust and hostile. 'El cántaro roto' is
written in the long but irregular lines which characterize many of

the poems of *La estación violenta*. It opens as the poet dreams of a world of 'vértigo y llama' where light and colours gyrate, opening vistas of promise and of repose. The sunflower, woods full of crystal sound, the wind, feathers, birds—all symbols of life and beauty—fill his imagination, and as he opens his eyes he sees the majesty of the night sky above him.

The poet then returns to reality and finds himself alone in an arid land, 'cactus, huizaches, piedras enormes que estallan bajo el sol'. The soil is barren, and the air threateningly brittle, as though existence itself is precarious; life is harsh, 'rumor de pies descalzos sobre el polvo', and even the pirú tree seems lifeless, 'como un surtidor petrificado'. The poet turns to this land of drought and pain, asking for some hope of transcendence:

¿no hay agua . . .?
¿No hay relinchos de caballos a la orilla del río, entre
   las grandes piedras redondas y relucientes . . .?
                                        (*Lib.* 233)

His rhetorical questions continue to assail the false promises of religions, Christianity having failed, as did the gods of fertility and regeneration of the Nahuas:

El dios-maíz, el dios-flor, el dios-agua, el dios-sangre,
   la Virgen,
¿todos se han muerto, se han ido, cántaros rotos al borde de la
   fuente cegada?   (*Lib.* 233-4)

He sees alive only forces of treachery and corruption, symbolized by the 'sapo verduzco' and by the treacherous chief who sold Moctezuma to Cortés—'¿ . . . sólo el cacique gordo de Cempoala es inmortal?' The images of the toad and the 'cacique gordo' blend into those of the conquering priest and lecherous capitalist[6] in a passage of subtle transition which deserves quotation in full:

Tendido al pie del divino árbol de jade regado con sangre,
   mientras dos esclavos jóvenes lo abanican,
en los días de las grandes procesiones al frente del pueblo,
   apoyado en la cruz: arma y bastón,
en traje de batalla, el esculpido rostro de sílex aspirando
   como un incienso precioso el humo de los fusilamentos,
los fines de semana en su casa blindada junto al mar, al lado de su querida cubierta de joyas de gas neón,
¿sólo el sapo es inmortal?
                                        (*Lib.* 234)

The rest of the poem falls into two parts: the first has three sections dramatically presenting suffering man against a specifically Mexican background of maguey and nopal, but universalized in the accumulation of aggressive acts in which man is victimized by nature—'la flor que sangra y hace sangrar . . . la noche que desuella con un pedernal invisible'—and by his fellow man:

> Oye a los huesos machacando a los huesos
> al tambor de piel humana golpeado por el fémur . . .
>
> (*Lib.* 234)

Man resists, however, and hope resists, 'Castillos interiores que incendia el pensamiento porque otro más puro se levante . . .', and the word still searches for lips to proclaim it. The poet turns to the broken pitcher to announce the rebirth of light and of speech, all symbolized in the life-giving powers of water, 'hasta que brote al fin el agua y crezca el árbol de anchas hojas de turquesa . . .'

The second part, which closes the poem, develops the theme of hope. The motifs of light and water, originally part of the sleeping poet's dream, now return, applied empirically to the world which can be created here and now. The solution is an active one, both spiritually and physically, since our dreams and desires must regain for us our lost paradise, but with labour and effort and especially with faith. If our dreams are strong enough we can will into existence our own resurrection, which will be in terms of mankind and humanity, 'el manantial para beber y mirarse y reconocerse y recobrarse . . .' (*Lib.* 235). For this we must dream back before the beginnings to the timelessness of myth, but a living myth in which life and death flow as the same stream, and in which we know ourselves as parts of the same whole in the unity of existence.[7]

The third poem with the title 'Intermitencias del Oeste' (*L.E.* 68–9), differs from 'El cántaro roto' in degree but not in kind. In the latter poem Paz shows old myths as forgotten and useless, while the corruption of the 'cacique gordo de Cempoalla' lives on in the 'fat cats' of today's Mexico. In 'Intermitencias del Oeste' he makes a more radical superimposition of earlier and present evils. The poem was written after the Olympic Games held in Mexico City in 1968, and, accompanied by a letter to the 'Señores Coordinadores del Programa Cultural de la XIX Olimpiada', was published in newspapers around the world. Paz had been asked to write a poem to commemorate the Games and had declined, until the uprisings and police reprisals. These produced both his poem and his resignation as Ambassador to India.

The central thread of the poem is the contrast between the clean whiteness of the paper before the poet, and the rage he feels, objectified only in the stain which the poem finally produces on the clarity of the page. Breaking this thread are interpolations in parentheses, and a central block of six lines in italics which stands out like the threat of a shamed country about to erupt in anger. The only lines which make clear the occasion of the poem are parenthesized and follow the italicized portion:

> (Los empleados
> Municipales lavan la sangre
> En la Plaza de los Sacrificios.)
>
> (*L.E.* 68)

This blood becomes linked with the stain of the poem itself in the closing lines:

> Mira ahora,
>   Manchada
> Antes de haber dicho algo
> Que valga la pena,
>   La limpidez.
>
> (*L.E.* 69)

The massacre of the students in fact took place before the Palacio de Bellas Artes, but Paz has transferred the horrific part of the Aztec rites to an incident in our own day to show that the bestial side of man is as constant as the spiritual. In effect, the degradation of the Nahuatl religion by the conquering Aztecs, who distorted the purity of the old beliefs to serve their political ends, is a process repeated in any faith or creed which compromises its ideals.

Chronologically speaking, the long and important 'Piedra de sol' follows *La estación violenta,* as it appeared in 1957 and is the last poem in the *Libertad bajo palabra* collection (237–54). 'Salamandra' is the penultimate poem in the volume of that name which first appeared in 1962 containing poems from 1958–61,[8] and is presumably a later work. However, 'Piedra de sol' shows Paz's ability to blend into one mythic substructure elements eclectically drawn from a variety of traditions, whereas 'Salamandra' is more committed to a distinctively Mexican background, and thus may claim first attention here. In the old legends the salamander was a type of lizard which could live in fire, and it is this regeneration through fire, with its connotations of spiritual initiation, which provides the central theme of the poem.

The complexities of the poem crystallize in the second half in a parenthetical narration of the story of Xólotl, the double of Quetzalcoatl, whose dog-shape represents the incarnation of matter, just as the Venus-identity of Quetzalcoatl, so obvious in 'Piedra de sol', represents pure spirit condemned to incarceration. Thus Quetzalcoatl among other things symbolizes the duality of spirit and matter, Xólotl being the victim whose sacrifice is necessary for the liberation of the spirit.[9] That this variant of the mythical hero is equivalent in Paz's mind with the poet is obvious here, as in the earlier 'Fuente' (*Lib.* 216–18),[10] since the poetic act is for Paz at once the result of spiritual initiation and suffering on the part of the poet, and his legacy of salvation to an insensitive world.

In the legends of the Nahuas as recounted in Laurette Séjourné's *Burning Water* (53–79), Quetzalcoatl was king of the ancient Toltecs, and perfect within human limitations, in the same way that King David represents to the Judaeo-Christian world the nearest human approximation to man before the Fall. Quetzalcoatl, whom one must assume to have had a historical existence, was wholly chaste until he was tricked by evil counsellors into getting drunk. In this state he committed a carnal act, the nature of which differs in the various tellings of the tale. In any case he repented of his sin to the extent of inflicting the most exacting penalties upon himself, abandoning his kingdom, and dying voluntarily by fire. But though his body burned, his spirit, like the salamander, remained undestroyed, and his heart rose to heaven to be transformed into the planet Venus, the female principle of love.

This transformation was not achieved without pain. Quetzalcoatl had first to visit the underworld in order to win his redemption, and he was either accompanied by or actually became his double, the dog Xólotl. Here again the myths diverge. In one legend Quetzalcoatl and Xólotl undertook a pilgrimage together in the underworld, suffering tests like those of Hercules. Quetzalcoatl, who was destined to inaugurate the fifth Sun or cosmic age, had to retrieve from the lord of the underworld, Mictlantecuhtli, the bones of the men destroyed as the fourth cosmic age ended, since with them he was to create the new race of mankind, that of which we are now a part. Even though Quetzalcoatl received the bones, he distrusted Mictlantecuhtli, who in anger sent quail in pursuit. Quetzalcoatl stumbled and fell, and the birds crumbled the bones, a disaster only redeemed by Quetzalcoatl's sacrificing himself on the bones which came to life as his blood fell on them. When the shackles of the body and matter were thus overcome, Quetzalcoatl as pure spirit could rise in the heavens as the planet Venus, which itself appears first as the evening star, then disappears for several days, reappearing in the east. Thus by the emergence of a spiritual force capable of freeing the world from inertia, the fifth era was inaugurated, the era of the Sun and of the Centre, that mystical fifth point of the quincunx which unifies the diversities of human experience objectified in the four cardinal points.

The other legend follows the path of Xólotl, though with the same pattern of suffering and redemption. As befits his baser nature, however, Xólotl's sacrifice is not the voluntary one of Quetzalcoatl. The legend tells that the sun had stopped its motion, and that all the gods decided that their death was needed to bring it back to life, that is to movement. Xólotl alone refused to die, and ran away to hide, first in the maize, then in the maguey. Pursued at every turn, he jumped into the water and became the axolotl fish, in which form he was finally caught and killed. His death released the spiritual force which, as the breath of Quetzalcoatl, set matter in motion again, or in higher terms allowed the creation of luminous energy or soul.

Paz combines elements of both legends in his return to the myth, or rather he tells both stories, so that Xólotl becomes doubly a symbol of sacrifice and redemption. First he tells of the flight and capture of Xólotl by the gods; secondly he describes Quetzalcoatl's underworld pilgrimage as made by Xólotl—a legitimate variation since they are two halves of the same entity, 'el dos-seres' —so that the penitent victim and the maker of men is Xólotl, 'el ojo reventado que llora por nosotros'. In some Nahuatl codices Xólotl is represented with a burst eye, which objectifies the 'sacrifice of the outer vision in order to concentrate on the inner, spiritual life'.[11] He is the 'doble de la Estrella', Venus, of course, 'La otra cara del Señor de la Aurora / Xólotl el ajolote'. With the word 'ajolote' (salamander) the gap is bridged, and the salamander motif reintroduced, the thematic structure of the poem now firmly established and rooted in the myths which lie at the heart of Nahuatl spirituality.

'Piedra de sol' (*Lib*. 237–54) comes directly from the rites of the Nahuas as far as its form is concerned, and in its structure of initiation and rebirth it draws upon Mexican tradition; but the universality of the paradigm begins to involve Paz in a wider frame of reference. The poem has 584 hendecasyllabic lines before the *da capo* ending which comes full circle to the beginning again, a number chosen to correspond with the 584 days of the cycle of the planet Venus. The symbolism of Venus in the Quetzalcoatl legend made the synodical revolutions of that planet the basis of astronomical and religious calculations throughout Central America.[12] The Venus years were computed in groups of five (corresponding to eight solar years), and five is the symbol for Venus, that is, for Quetzalcoatl, as well as being the unifying centre of the quincunx. Thus the Nahuatl Era, 'Ollin Tonatiuh', was the fifth era or the fifth Sun, and the Aztec calendar stone, with the face of the sun in the centre, is the astronomical record of the previous four eras through which the world had passed before the emergence of Quetzalcoatl-Venus. Thus the cyclical form of the poem objectifies the view of creation of so-called primitive peoples who stand outside the history-bound, linear time of modern man. Paz, in *Corriente alterna* (205–12), has developed his feeling that the cultural revolution of today is bringing to an end the unnatural era of 'rectilinear' time, ruled by the idea of progress, and reinstituting the feeling of cyclical time which is most germane to the nature of man himself. 'Piedra de sol', whose form is its content, is perhaps the most forceful affirmation of this intuition.

'Piedra de sol' is an *anima* poem, in the sense that its thematic constant is the 'inherited collective image of woman . . . in a man's unconscious, with the help of which he apprehends the nature of woman'.[13] This collective image of woman blends with the female principles of the universe, so that the search for regeneration through passion and through the unknown forces of the cosmos becomes one and the same. The epigraph from Nerval's 'Arthémis' emphasizes at once the uniqueness of each moment of love and its ever-repeating rhythm, like the planet Venus, which returns always renewed, but always the same.

The poem opens in a landscape which represents the poet's illuminated state of mind, perhaps in a dream sequence where elements of nature most evocative of tranquillity and promise blend:

> un sauce de cristal, un chopo de agua,
> un alto surtidor que el viento arquea,
> un árbol bien plantado mas danzante,
> un caminar de río que se curva . . .
> *(Lib.* 237)

The poet's awareness of present vision and of the future possibility of unknown evils is objectified by a journey during which he is met by 'una presencia como un canto súbito', and the merging of the theme of spiritual peregrination with that of erotic love takes him through knowledge of woman into a new realm of awareness:

> el mundo ya es visible por tu cuerpo,
> es transparente por tu transparencia . . .
> *(Lib.* 238)

Verbs of motion keep alive the feeling of double pilgrimage—'Voy por tu cuerpo como por el mundo'—and as woman becomes identified with outer reality, she assumes the properties of fertility and regeneration, corn and water:

> tu falda de maíz ondula y canta,
> tu falda de cristal, tu falda de agua . . .[14]
> *(Lib.* 239)

The encounter ends in 'un abismo brusco', and the poet's steps now enter 'corredores sin fin de la memoria', a house of melancholy and neglect as opposed to the openness and natural beauty of the landscape of love. His path takes him through avenues of mirrors which repeat back to him the sterility of his own image until he breaks into an invocation to womankind, from the girls leaving school at five o'clock to the adolescent leaning on the balcony:

> he olvidado tu nombre, Melusina,
> Laura, Isabel, Perséfona, María . . .
> *(Lib.* 240)

To encompass all women Paz casts his net of allusions wide. In French mythology Melusina was a water-nymph married to a mortal, and allowed to return to her former state, half-woman, half-serpent, once a week, as long as she kept this secret. Spied on by her husband, she had to flee in her nymph shape, and could thereafter only haunt the places where she had lived as a human. Melusina is one of the figures which come to the mind of Nadja, the heroine of André Breton's novel of the same title; for the Surrealists her dual nature represented woman's unifying character and instinctive contact with a primitive world—like Eve, Melusina holds knowledge dangerous to man.[15] The connotations of 'Laura' and 'Isabel' are wide and include, at least, shades of Petrarch and Garcilaso de la Vega; 'Perséfona' looks back to Greek mythology in which she was the queen of the underworld; 'María' of all names has echoes too far-reaching to need comment. The 'reina de serpientes' is the Aztec Mother Goddess, Coatlicue, whose skirt was made of intertwined snakes, but the Mexican allusion is only part of this eclectic evocation of the mysteries of the female principle.

Images and metaphors again identify woman with Nature, sometimes menacing, even lethal, but always regenerative in her function both as unifier of opposites and as reconciler of antagonisms:

> terraza del jazmín, sal en la herida,
> ramo de rosas para el fusilado,
> nieve en agosto, luna del patíbulo . . .
>
> (*Lib.* 241)

But there is a long, lonely road from the awareness of womanhood incarnate to her whose glance will create the instant of perception which brings release. The poet, alone with only dreams to defend him against 'el mundo con su horario carnicero', finds himself in the nether world of suffering and self-sacrifice which precedes all transcendence. He enters a realm of alienation and cruelty, of threatening death and bitter existence, and he is led, like so many a hero in the initiatory stages, painfully and haltingly 'hacia el centro del círculo', a way filled with spiritual anguish and even physical pain. Melusina appears again, the keeper of secret knowledge, the serpent-woman whom man should never see, but who curses with forbidden knowledge those who do see her.

This underworld journey of the soul again finds its objective correlative in the pilgrimage of Quetzalcoatl, who also sought and gained hidden knowledge incarnate in woman, as the figure of Melusina is replaced by 'los dos ojos / de una niña ahogada hace mil años'. One version of Quetzalcoatl's sin describes him as having been made drunk by demons led by an evil spirit, Tezcatlipoca, who brought him a whore called Xochiquetzal. Xochiquetzal was in fact goddess of prostitutes and of love, and identical with the

Great Mother of the Universe. Thus, in gaining carnal knowledge of Xochiquetzal, Quetzalcoatl regressed into Xochipilli, the son-lover of the Mother Goddess.[16] The layers of interconnections of the serpent-woman, Melusina, with Eve, and now with the Mother Goddess, also with all the taboos of incest basic to primitive societies[17] and brilliantly challenged in Paz's lines, take us deeper and deeper into the collective unconscious where the myth of the cosmic return never disappears:

> mirada madre de la niña sola
> que ve en el padre grande un hijo niño,
> miradas que nos miran desde el fondo
> de la vida y son trampas de la muerte
> — ¿o es al revés: caer en esos ojos
> es volver a la vida verdadera?
>
> (*Lib.* 244)

From this point of enlightenment and oneness with the universal being the poet can return to grasp the eternal in the passing moment of daily life, and his memory becomes specific—Christopher Street, la Reforma, Oaxaca, the Hotel Vernet, moments and places where his own experience has given him knowledge of fulfilment. In even more brusque juxtaposition follow memories of Madrid in 1937, when war brought final fragmentation to a disrupted universe, and the immediate defence of man in search of wholeness and communion:

> torres hendidas, frentes esculpidas
> y el huracán de los motores, fijo:
> los dos se desnudaron y se amaron
> por defender nuestra porción eterna
> nuestra ración de tiempo y paraíso,
> tocar nuestra raíz y recobrarnos . . .
>
> (*Lib.* 246)

Love is man's defence against death, against division, against the routine of daily life, against all the corruptions and hypocrisies which separate us from each other and from ourselves. It is the freedom of the soul from all the forces which seek to dehumanize mankind, and ultimately it provides the gateway to an even higher transcendence at the heart of which stands

> lo que llamamos Dios, el ser sin nombre . . .
> plentitud de presencias y de nombres . . .
>
> (*Lib.* 249)

The circle must be completed, so the pilgrimage continues, as the verbs of motion reappear—'sigo mi desvarío . . . camino . . . subo y bajo . . .' Then the poet is alone no longer, 'tú a mi lado / caminas', and the good things are his once more: trees, rivers, corn, birds, squirrels, laughter, and the moment of union in which time is transcended.

In contrast there is history and its useless sacrifice, and the poet searches for meaning in a world gallery of murders and stupidities, from the tragedies of Agamemnon, Socrates, Brutus, Moctezuma, to Robespierre, Churruca, Lincoln, Trotski, and Madero, all absurdities of a world full of division, ignoring humanity. There is no escape from time once we have surrendered our lives and ourselves to it; and there is no recall for a life once wasted. The only defence is unity, so that through awareness of the Being of which we are a part we can transcend the limitations of our separate identities:

> para que pueda ser he de ser otro,
> salir de mi, buscarme entre los otros,
> los otros que no son si yo no existo,
> los otros que me dan plena existencia . . .
> (*Lib.* 252)

Thirst for totality returns him to woman as reconciler of divisions and harmonizer of opposites:

> Eloísa, Perséfona, María,
> muestra tu rostro al fin para que vea
> mi cara verdadera, la del otro,
> mi cara de nosotros siempre todos . . .
> (*Lib.* 252)

Woman contains all contraries, as day and night unite in the symbol of Hecate,[18] 'señora de la noche, / torre de claridad, reina del alba, / virgen lunar'. Hecate was the daughter of Zeus, who gave her power over the heavens, the earth, and the waters. She was equated with Persephone and also with Artemis, the twin sister of Apollo, god of light, and herself goddess of the moon. Nerval's archetypal woman and Paz's blend as the circle begins to close. Of her the poet asks that he emerge to the new birth of undifferentiated being beyond the night of selfhood, to the realm of cosmic unity in which 'yo soy tú somos nosotros, / al reino de pronombres enlazados . . .'

The pilgrimage and the illumination seem to end in a return from the 'indecible presencia de presencias'; however, the return is not an end, but a new beginning. Man's existence, like Nature, is cyclical, and experience is regenerative, so that though he returns to his own consciousness, the poet feels that the barriers of the self are broken, and cannot completely close again:

> todas las puertas se desmoronaban
> y el sol entraba a saco por mi frente. . .
> *(Lib.* 254)

The sun superimposes once again the levels of spiritual awareness and of physical sunshine, so that the poet once again opens his eyes on the landscape where his original awakening took place:

> un sauce de cristal, un chopo de agua,
> un alto surtidor que el viento arquea,
> un árbol bien plantado mas danzante,
> un caminar de río que se curva,
> avanza, retrocede, da un rodeo
> y llega siempre:
> *(Lib.* 254)

The circle is not closed, however, for with the awareness gained the poet is no longer the self which began the pilgrimage; this is a spiral, not a circular trajectory, back to the starting-place, but now transformed by the experience which is the poem itself.

'Piedra de sol' at first glance seems the most complex of Paz's poems, but this is not in fact the case. Its form is 'closed' in the sense that its lines are uniform in length and their number determined by an external consideration, the synodical revolution of Venus, rather than by the demands of the poem itself. It draws upon a frame of reference, both mythological and historical, far wider than most of Paz's poems, so that the diversity of its motifs dazzles, and requires the reader to grasp unusual analogies. The closed form of the poem is natural, since eroticism tends towards ceremony; outer reality must be transformed into symbols in order to set up the system of correspondences by which language can express the analogy between a couple and the world. Paz's correspondences are almost an *embarras de richesses*, but his basic analogy is starkly simple, because all its seeming complexities lead back to the centre, the act of love as a rite of passage from a limited consciousness to a transcendent awareness of cosmic harmony.

Harmony of whatever kind requires previous experience of discord, or, in mythical terms, rebirth must follow initiation. The consciousness cannot know expansion if it has not previously been tested and its endurance stretched. This is the structure on which the poem rests, and its spiral form points out the eternity of this truth. For the poet the poem itself is the objective correlative of this same experience; it bears witness to the re-emergence of language, when passion and art have struggled with its insufficiencies to express what is really inexpressible.

TRADITIONAL MYTH AND CHANGING STYLE

In style and motif 'Solo a dos voces' (*Sal.* 109–15) shows a change in Paz's aesthetics when compared with the poems of *Libertad bajo palabra*, though its structure marks it unmistakably as his. 'Salamandra' already shows stylistic differences from earlier poems, yet its abundance of thematic motifs somewhat lessens the impact of its form. 'Solo a dos voces' introduces the terse dynamic poetry of *Ladera Este*, and since this study is concerned with the polyphonic relationship in Paz's poetry between the constant centre and the evolving periphery, this appears a convenient juncture for a discussion of the differences which an uninitiated reader would find in juxtaposing, for instance, 'El cántaro roto' and 'Piedra de sol' of the preceding section with 'Solo a dos voces'.

It is not that Paz's work up to 1957 was in any way bound by traditional versification. There is great variety of line length and rhythm throughout *Libertad bajo palabra*, and very few poems strictly adhere to formal patterns. The most homogeneous group is that of poems belonging to *La estación violenta* (1957), in which Paz uses lines of verse of anything from two to fifty syllables to give his poems an epic solemnity. The demands of reading such poems aloud enforce a rhythm which is continuous and majestic like the waves of the sea. Contrast is achieved by varying the line length, but the contrast emphasizes the basic continuity of phrases, since the reader strains always for the end of the line, the voice rising and falling at commas but remaining even in its flow as the eye moves horizontally. The result is an accumulative rhythm of phrases within each line, and of lines within each section; a density of thought reflected in image after image, rising to a climax and falling in cadence—an awe-inspiring verbal and imagistic structure:

> y sea el alma el llano después del incendio, el pecho lunar
> de un mar petrificado que no refleja nada
> sino la extensión extendida, el espacio acostado sobre sí mismo,
>   las alas inmensas desplegadas,
> y sea todo como la llama que se esculpe y se hiela en la roca de
>   entrañas transparentes,
> duro fulgor resuelto ya en cristal y claridad pacífica.
>
> Y el río remonta su curso, repliega sus velas, recoge sus
>   imágenes y se interna en sí mismo.
>
> 'El río', Lib. 232)

'Piedra de sol' by contrast is like a technical *recogimiento*. The wide range of motifs and the unusual transitions from one to another, as well as the cosmic theme of love and the female principle, seem to have imposed on Paz not economy but strictness of versification. The palindrome form is of course more obvious given an unvaried line, and the background of a regular syllable-count allows for more concentration on the subtle new meanings which the experiences of the poem bestow upon the apparent 'return home' of the ending. Since the ear becomes accustomed to the predictable quality of the hendecasyllable, the thematic content of the poem achieves a limited but dramatic independence in keeping with the spiritual pilgrimage of the poet-narrator. Experience is objectified in images, and the whole poem is a gigantic metaphor from which neither eye nor ear is distracted by formal innovations. Though it is a vast generalization, it seems valid to describe Paz's poetry up to 1957 as dependent upon rhythm and image.

'Solo a dos voces' is quite another matter, however. The aesthetic basis of this poetry has shifted to the word, and more specifically, the syllable, as the Mexican background receives one patina after another from French, English, and North American influences. The emergence of the poem was always a central preoccupation for Paz, but it becomes now less the break-through of the Muse than the painful extraction of signs and their meanings and a questioning of the basis of trust upon which language as a phenomenon rests. This concern is typical of his work in the 60s, and he has an amazing ability to discuss it discursively. He sees the course of modern poetry as having been set by Mallarmé and the 'poema crítico', which is his definition of 'Un coup de dés', and about which he says:

Poema crítico: si no me equivoco, la unión de estas dos palabras contradictorias quiere decir: aquel poema que contiene su propia negación y que hace de esa negación el punto de partida del canto, a igual distancia de afirmación y negación. La poesía, concebida por Mallarmé como la única posibilidad de identificación del lenguaje con lo absoluto, de ser el absoluto, se niega a sí misma cada vez que se realiza en un poema (ningún acto, inclusive un acto puro e hipotético: sin autor, tiempo ni lugar, abolirá el azar)—salvo si el poema es simultáneamente crítica de esa tentativa. La negación de la negación anula el absurdo y disuelve el azar. El poema, el acto de arrogar los dados o pronunciar el número que suprimirá el azar (porque sus cifras coincidirán con la totalidad), es absurdo y no lo es . . .[19]

So the thematic pivot of 'Solo a dos voces' is that moment of paralysis which precedes all creative activity, the death which prepares for rebirth. But the work is a fascinating complex of superimposed motifs, the unravelling of which necessarily destroys its elliptical synthesis. The poem's occasion is the winter solstice, but the epigraph quotes Corominas's *Diccionario crítico-etimológico*: 'En ninguna otra lengua occidental son tantas las palabras fantasmas.' And so the equation is established. The cosmic cycle must reach a nadir of gestation before new life can begin; similarly words are signs which can die and yet be revived by the complicity which gives them meaning in human commerce. Language is both the poet's tool and his final product; it is the lifeline which pulls man from chaos, the means by which form, order, and sense are created and affirmed. And so it is not merely the choice of words which becomes important, but the use of them as epistemological tools to define the reality which their improper use can distort and belie. This understanding of the creative power of the word produces a concern with objects as parts of reality, even as man himself is part of the natural world. Man has his place in the total structure, and all is open to exploration: the word, the object, man, the metaphysical nature of all these things. Thus in 'Solo a dos voces' the drop of water falling while the poet writes has a validity in itself—'Ella cae y yo escribo'—and is not merely an objective correlative for the poet's inner processes.

Such an attempt to clarify the word and thereby to restore importance to the object seems part of the poetic atmosphere of our time. One recalls the efforts of Francis Ponge to create a language pure enough to be accurate in its reflection of the world, and not distorted by the 'lugubrious and often masochistic preoccupation with ideology that has characterized so much of Western literature'.[20] Ponge's poetry, for instance, 'Le Soleil lu à la radio',[21] affirms the power of language to direct thought and create false emotion, and warns of the need to restore to the word its primal power. Charles Olson in the early 50s was expressing similar ideas when, in his essay 'Projective Verse',[22] he coined the word 'objectism', defined as

. . . the getting rid of the lyrical interference of the individual as ego, of the 'subject' and his soul, that peculiar presumption by which western man has interposed himself between what he is as a creature of nature (with certain instructions to carry out) and those other creations of nature which we may, with no derogation, call objects.[23]

To name is to create, and the responsibility is a heavy one, so that language must be subject to constant doubt and scrutiny. The most critical of Latin America's contemporary poets, Nicanor Parra, finds validity only in words which he has 'invented' by peeling away all layers of conventional hypocrisy and double meaning:

Conforme: os invito a quemar vuestras naves,
Como los fenicios pretendo formarme mi propio alfabeta.[24]

Parra polishes and refines his language until it is newly made to his satisfaction and as hard-edged as a sword. But as the creator names and brings the poem into being, so he is himself created as artist by the language he has chosen and remade. The cycle is complete; the act of negation has become that of affirmation—the poem.

This double process of affirmation and negation lies behind the counterpoint of the dictionary and the poem itself which forms the nexus of 'Solo a dos voces'. The dead forms exist; and the power of creation also exists—in the intuition of the poet whose magic is needed to give the life-breath. Yet this poetic intuition needs the bridge of words in order to define itself, and the anguish of this process is obvious in the almost stuttering opening lines. Here the monosyllabic 'Si', 'No', and the repetitious motifs—'mundo', 'presente', 'solsticio', 'invierno'—draw together the near-paralysis of the winter solstice with that of the poet, whose power over the dead pages of the dictionary almost succumbs in the struggle with the inertia of outworn words. 'Trabajos del poeta' of 1949[25] uses

surrealistic images and free associations to express this same
bitter, yet for Paz inevitable, battle, sometimes objectifying it in a
warlike confrontation of poet and word. The truncated phrases,
unpunctuated lines, staccato monosyllables of 'Solo a dos voces'
have lost facility, but therefore strike a more powerful blow:

> Si decir No
> Al mundo al presente
> Hoy (solsticio de invierno)
> No es decir
> > Si
> Decir es solsticio de invierno
> Hoy en el mundo
> > > No
> Es decir
> > Si
> Decir mundo presente
> No es decir
> > > ¿Qué es
> Mundo Solsticio Invierno?
> ¿Qué es decir?
> > > > (Desde hace horas
> Oigo caer, en el patio negro
> Una gota de agua.
> Ella cae y yo escribo.)   (*Sal.* 109)

The parenthesized lines here, and in alternating sequence
throughout the poem, return to the actual moment of the poem's
creation. That is, the object created, as it might seem in retrospect,
is never allowed to separate itself from the process of creation, in
which are fused the poet (who must imprison words upon a page
and be imprisoned there by them), the ink, and the dripping of
water, symbol of fertility about to return to a dead land.

The next section turns from the earth to the heavens; above the
black, sterile soil is the fixed globe of the sun, and the image of the
'sol parado' recalls a moment in the legend of Xólotl, which Paz
used in the poem 'Salamandra'. Like the sun, the poet sits

> (. . . A la mitad del pensamiento
> Me quedo, como el sol,
> Parado
> En la mitad de mí,
> Separado.)   (*Sal.* 110)

The sacrifice of a redeemer will set the sun to rights, but the poet, 'separado' now, not 'parado', not halted, but divided in himself, must find the sacrificial victim in his own entrails.

Mythologies change, but the paradigm is the same, as it is now Ceres who must be brought back to life by offerings. The virgins who bring these merge with the alliterations of the dictionary world, which is also revived by the creative spirit:

> Mundo mondo,
> Sonaja de semillas semánticas:
>
> Vírgenes móndigas.
>
> *(Sal. 110)*

The concept of rebirth has many forms, as the procession of the virgins bearing bread to Mother Earth—'Como una corona cándida / La canasta del pan'—and the communion bread of the 'Pascua de Resurrección' become as one image of sacrifice and redemption. This too blends into the image of woman the life-giver:

> Altar vivo los pechos,
> Sobre mesa de tierra vasos de sol:
> Como y bebo, hombre soy.
>
> *(Sal. 111)*

Here the poet enters the mythological realm of the Earth Mother, worshipped as the universal Genetrix, the source and promise of life itself.[26] The actual ceremonies of the Terra Mater in many religions have involved women, and there has been a close symbolic association of woman with the land, and of the sexual act with the processes of agriculture. This is the association which carries over into the following parenthesized segment, where the 'sonaja' re-appears, now to describe the poem—'sonaja de simientes'. The image and the alliteration draw the equation between the poem and the world ('sonaja de semillas semánticas'), and the image of the seed links the life-force of the man to that within the poem, to that of the universal fire ('El grano de fuego / En el cuerpo de Ceres'), and back again to the moment of creation, the drop of ink forming the word on the page, and the water dripping in the patio. The blackness of the ink recalls the 'diosa negra', Kali, the creating-destroying goddess of India who becomes a familiar figure in *Ladera Este.*[27]

'Solo a dos voces' pays homage to the presence of Kali, and the opposing motifs of black and white reappear throughout ('la tierra negra y blanca . . .'), but it is the life-force which dominates the imagery. The fertilizing power of the drops of ink and of water re-echo in the sexually significant image of the horse, which again blends the potency of natural forces with the power of the word on the page:

> (. . . Dibujar un caballo de agua
> Dibujar en la página
> Un caballo de yerba . . .)
> (*Sal.* 111)

These images of sublimated energy announce the turning-point, for as the cockerel crows the sun awakens to life. The imagined procession of virgins breaks into sound and movement—'Voces y risas, baile y panderos'—compared with wind and water, traditional symbols of the life-force. Once again the complexity of images suggests the sexual act, now in the conception of new life in the womb:

> Muchachas,
>   Cántaros penantes,
> El agua se derrama,
> El vino se derrama,
> El fuego se derrama,
> Penetra las entrañas,
> La piedra se despierta:
> Lleva un sol en el vientre.
> Como el pan en el horno,
> El hijo de la piedra incandescente
> Es el hijo de nadie.
> (*Sal.* 112)

A new parenthesis breaks this thread with the parallel theme of the poet and his dictionary which he now shakes like a 'ramo seco', while the vision of joy and celebration fades away outside in the 'humedad y cemento' of his patio.

The section which follows is a pivotal one in that both themes, that of the winter solstice and that of the dictionary, are pulled together into the mythical pattern of the search for origins which leads ultimately to regeneration and rebirth.[28] In inverse direction the poet flicks over the pages of the dictionary where unused words lie waiting, and the alliteration and the nonsensical conjunctions

produce the effect of an incantation, or a chant in some foreign
tongue:

> . . . 'sofisma, símil, selacio, salmo,
> Rupestre, rosca, ripio, réprobo,
> Rana, Quito, quejido,
> Pulque, ponzoña, picotín, peluca . . .'

Man is drawn back towards the source, to the moment of transcendence where unity of vision is achieved, and the black goddess
is accepted and acknowledged:

> Simiente,
>   Gota de energía,
> Joya verde
> Entre los pechos negros de la diosa.

None the less, the creative process will always demand vigilance
and pain, as the poet must set himself against the easy con-
ventionalism of words, 'contra la corriente, / Contra la aguja
hipnotizada / Y los sofismos del cuadrante'. But if the cycle of
inertia is overcome, if the act of naming becomes a purification,
'mondadura', then the heart of the vortex may be reached, and the
illusory agitation of meaningless communication avoided:

> No el movimiento del círculo,
> Maestro de espejismos:
>   La quietud
> En el centro del movimiento.

(Sal. 114)

The sacrificial act must continue—'Decir es penitencia de palabras'
—and the union of opposites unpretentiously sought:

> La zona negra y blanca,
> El húmedo cemento, el patio,
> El no saber qué digo
> Entre la ausencia y la presencia
> De este mundo . . .

(Sal. 114)

Memory is man's guide-line, 'raíz en la tiniebla', yet not even here
may the poet find security, for the cup must be emptied to the
dregs, and darkness and oblivion also accepted:

> Come tiniebla,
>   Come olvido:
> No lo que dices, lo que olvidas,
> Es lo que dices:

With this resignation, resignation which is its own triumph, the poem comes full circle. The world is still at the solstice, it still awaits light and movement, and it still symbolizes the poet, whose self is divided in the suffering of the creative act:

> Hoy es solsticio de invierno
> En el mundo
> Hoy estás separado
> En el mundo
> Hoy es el mundo
> Ánima en pena en el mundo.

Yet, as in 'Piedra de sol', the circle cannot finally close, for the poem now exists as rebirth and affirmation. To paraphrase Paz himself: from the lifeless pages of the dictionary, and from the nadir of non-being, words and intuitions have been drawn into that zone of vibrations where signs achieve their own tension and independent existence.[29]

MYTHS OF INDIA

In 1962 Octavio Paz was appointed Ambassador to India, and took up residence in New Delhi. With the single exception of 'Cuento de dos jardines', all the poems in *Ladera Este* (Mexico, 1969) were written in India, Afghanistan, or Ceylon. They take the reader into a new world of unfamiliar landscapes, history, and myth, so that for the first time Paz has footnoted his own poems, 'con el temor (¿la esperanza?) de que estas notas, lejos de disiparlos, aumenten los enigmas.'[30] The poems do not become less a testimony of Paz himself; rather the atmosphere of the collection changes. Approximately two-thirds of the poems reflect to a greater or lesser degree the poet's assimilation of new surroundings and new influences, whereas the remainder are intense, direct, and completely personal. Of the larger group, some, such as 'Cochin' (*L.E.* 46), are more or less occasional pieces, reflections brought to mind by what the poet has happened upon either in Nature or in human behaviour. There are others, an important group, which depend upon concepts, usually from Tantric or Mahayana Buddhist philosophies, which cause the poet to react, modifying or elucidating them in line with his own metaphysics. Such poems as 'Lectura de John Cage' and 'Vrindaban', 'Sunyata' and 'Maithuna' show this process at work. In 'Domingo en la isla de Elefanta' and

'Viento entero' the Indian gods Shiva and Parvati appear, used symbolically for varying effects, a more or less superficial type of allusion. But in another group, which includes 'Al pintor Swaminathan', 'El día en Udaipur', and the ironic 'Golden Lotuses' series, the analogies between Paz's own concepts and those of the Hindu beliefs become clearer and deeper. In all these poems, like a diver in search of pearls, Paz explores the realms of mythology and religion, understanding the beliefs which men have systematized in them, and taking from them the symbols and the patterns which fit the structure of his own poetic vision. This he does not distort; he is not swept into new currents, nor does he find Oriental faiths more convincing to him as a religious being than Christianity. His epistemological quest continues, but where traditional patterns coincide with his own thought, he enriches his work with what they can give him. Hence the complex suggestiveness of many of the poems in this volume, where compression and economy of language have coincided with profound thought, the whole filtered through Paz's particular poetic intuition.

The poems which provide the most concrete analogies with Paz's earlier work are those which draw on the Indian version of the Earth Mother myth. 'Al pintor Swaminathan' (*L.E.* 22–3) begins with the process of creation and ends with the created object itself. It passes through the colours, the shapes, and the raw materials from which the painting emerges 'Contra el rostro en blanco del mundo'. The creative act of the painter becomes that of every artist, all a part of the gigantic sacrifice which creation entails, as the drop of ink becomes blood and then honey: 'La gota de tinta de sangre de miel'. The motif of blood-redness carries the theme into the heart of the paradox of cosmic creation, where the principles of creation and destruction exist side by side:

> Salta el rojo mexicano
> > Y se vuelve negro
> Salta el rojo de la India
> > Y se vuelve negro
> Los labios ennegrecen
> > Negro de Kali
> > (*L.E.* 23)

Connotations of Aztec sacrifices in which blood was shed to feed the sun, fountain of life, thus shade into the symbolism of red and

black in Indian mythology. Here the colour red carries also the
symbolism of creative energy, the other side of the coin of sacrifice,
as for Paz the poem emerges from the suffering of the poet, or, as
in the Indian pantheon, one of the avatars of Devi, Shiva's consort,
is Kali, the Black Goddess.

In the traditions of Brahmanism,[31] the great god Shiva and his
spouse, Parvati, or Devi, among others of her names, are the first
dualization of the neuter Brahman, the creative power sent by the
Absolute, Vishnu, to recreate the universe at the dawn of each
kalpa, or Brahman-day. The male and female principles are the
pair of opposites which together are one essence. They cannot be
at variance, for the goddess expresses Shiva's secret nature, and
her character is an extension of his. Inevitably this goddess takes
on the characteristics of the universal Mother Goddess worshipped
in pre-Aryan times as giver of life and energy, Shakti-Maya, the
form-giving dynamic power, and in Shivaite Tantra philosophy
she is the incarnation of the divine energy of the Absolute. Yet
there is a destructive power also at work in the universe, equally
vital, counterbalancing the creative as death balances life. This is
Kali, the Black Goddess, *kali* being the feminine form of the word
kala, meaning 'time'. Indian art depicts Kali standing in a boat
that floats on an ocean of blood, or adorned with the dripping
heads and limbs of her victims, dancing on the prostrate body of
her holy consort, Shiva, her only beloved. The female principle,
the great Earth Mother, is a composite symbol just as life itself is
composed of the light and the dark, or as minds function both on
the conscious and on the unconscious level. Parvati (Devi) and
Kali are the two halves of Shakti-Maya, the constantly creating-
destroying goddess.

That Paz's ideology includes an awareness of the *anima* is
obvious from his earliest poems onward. The female principle as
creator and renewer of life appears and reappears in all his poetry,
seeming to provide him with a key to the secrets of the source of
energy in the cosmos and in the mind of man himself. Shakti-
Maya, the giver of forms, inspirer of the life-force, manifesting
herself in all forms of the Great Goddess, and in woman herself,
is a familiar presence in Paz's poetry. Moreover, the cycle of
sacrifice preceding creation, the Kali manifestation of Shakti-
Maya, is Paz's own conception of the poetic function, as is so
clearly symbolized in 'Fuente' (*Lib.* 216–18), in which the poet

must offer himself in sacrifice in order that the poem be released, or in the death of Xólotl to restore life to the sun in 'Salamandra'. Death and rebirth, destruction and creation, are necessary parts of the same process for Paz as for Indian mythology. In psychological terms, the dark side of the mind, the unconscious, Kali, must be acknowledged so that the creative act may take place in total harmony.

The essence of the poem to Swaminathan is the concept of creative rebirth. The red of creation is also the red of sacrifice, and Kali must receive homage as the picture emerges with its potent colours:

> El amarillo y sus fieras abrasadas
> El ocre y sus tambores subterráneos
> El cuerpo verde de la selva negra . . .
>
> (L.E. 23)

The propitiation of light and dark, of conscious and unconscious, is what inspires the image of 'el sexo de la Guadalupe', startling to the Western mind, which has kept immaculate its conception of the Blessed Mother, leaving on the outside walls of its cathedrals, as Zimmer observes, its 'hell-brood' and its gargoyles.[32] Paz, however, responds to the fuller concept of a Great Goddess, Mother of Creation, in which opposites are synthesized, and the dialectic of life and death, good and evil, sacrifice and creation, is harmonized into a peace which, for him, is not a religious but an aesthetic absolute—the work of art, at once enigma and answer:

> El cuadro es un cuerpo
> Vestido sólo por su enigma desnudo . . .
>
> (L.E. 23)

'El día en Udaipur' (L.E. 25–8), anchored in space and time by a specific occasion and place, is, like the Hindu myths, a dialectic moving towards synthesis. In it, as is often the case in Ladera Este, the poem moves from the diversity of outward appearances to a unity, be it of man and Nature, of lover and beloved, or of the poet and his creation. Because of this instinctive movement towards non-differentiation, the Indian religious forms can lend themselves to Paz, even though his ideology rejects the scope of their transcendental ideas. The non-dualistic breadth of Mahayana Buddhism and Tantra in particular coincides with his resolution of paradox in the poem and in the act of love.

As it presents itself on the page, 'El día en Udaipur' is a dialogue. Groups of five lines follow each other, each group divided into three lines on the left of the page and two on the right, question and answer, or comment and counter-comment. So it is that the literary tradition of the Tantra conceives of the never-ending dialogue between Shiva and his consort, each alternately teaching and being taught. Through their dialogue the secret essence of the Brahman, the Two-in-One, is brought within the realm of human understanding. It is the harmony of opposites in some greater whole which inspires this poem, occasioned by the sight of the rococo palaces and teeming bazaar of Udaipur, in Northern India.

Both the visual and the conceptual contrasts appear in the opening lines—the white palace beside the black lake, *lingam* and *yoni*, the phallic symbol of Shiva, and the sexual symbol of the great goddess. It is night, and as Parvati enfolds Shiva, the poet feels surrounded by the vast, impersonal majesty of the heavens, yet secure in his humanity:

> Estrellas inhumanas.
> Pero la hora es nuestra.
>   (*L.E.* 25)

Dawn breaks as he asserts the duality of man, body and spirit, with all the infinite possibilities this leaves him heir to:

> Caigo y me elevo,
> Ardo y me anego. ¿Sólo
> Tienes un cuerpo?
>   (*L.E.* 25)

The palaces gleam white as the sun gains strength, and the human turmoil begins to fill the bazaar. All is activity, energy, the myriad changing forms of Shakti-Maya, yet death and sacrifice are there too: the lamb to be slaughtered for Kali, Kali herself dancing on the body of Shiva, the dark side and the light combined in a full acceptance of all creation, so that

> Del mismo plato comen
> Dioses, hombres y bestias.
>   (*L.E.* 27)

As evening replaces the day, the poem's rhythm slows, short vowels are replaced by long, and sibilants lengthen lines and draw them nearer silence:

... Encienden
Luces sobre las aguas.
Ondulaciones . . .

(*L.E.* 27)

The poet and the woman, opposites seeking each other, form one
whole in Nature, one spark of life against the void, one part of
the universal life-force:

Viva balanza:
Los cuerpos enlazados
Sobre el vacío
El cielo nos aplasta,
El agua nos sostiene.

(*L.E.* 27)

The poem ends with an ambiguity reminiscent of the riddles of
Zen Buddhism:

Esto que he visto y digo
El sol, blanco, lo borra.

(*L.E.* 28)

As an agent of time itself, controlling our lives, the sun will move
to its next cycle and cancel out today's existence; yet in so far as
white contains all colours, so perhaps the reader is to interpret the
sun as a symbol of the Absolute resolving all paradoxes and
containing all antitheses in a timeless truth. The poem exists, after
all, as man's defence against time, or perhaps his testimony to the
harmony of opposites which has been its theme.

In a different vein are the three poems called 'Golden Lotuses'
(1), (2), and (3) (*L.E.* 30, 32, and 34 respectively), in which the
ironic tone acts as an antidote to the sublime connotations of the
title.[33] According to the legends, when Vishnu, the divine life
substance, prepares to put forth the universe at the start of each
kalpa, or Brahman-day, there issues from his navel a lotus which
is the duplicate manifestation of the goddess Lotus at his feet. The
lotus is thousand-petalled and is gold, symbolizing the uncorrupted
nature of this first product of the creative principle. In the centre
of the lotus is Brahma, the four-faced God-Creator of the Universe, at whose command the visible and created world then
emerges, mountains first, from the pericarp of the lotus. Vishnu,
during the night of Brahma, has been sleeping on the cosmic
ocean; in the Hindu conception the waters of this ocean are

female, and the lotus flower is their generative organ. And so the cosmic lotus, by extension the lotus goddess, Padma, the spouse of Vishnu, becomes identified with the creative aspect of Earth, or the Terra Mater, a local development of the pre-Aryan Great Mother Goddess. The lotus is a sign of her presence, and according to Zimmer, she is the greatest power in the Orient today.[34]

The women who occasion the 'Golden Lotuses' are treated in ironic but not irreverent fashion. They are like fallen goddesses, or perhaps the Kali side which lies within every Earth Mother figure, and therefore within woman herself and every woman as well. In the first poem the lady is deadly and inhuman, making love not with warmth or passion, but coldly:

> La descarga del gimnoto
> O, más bien, el chasquido
> De la seda
>   Al rasgarse.
>   (*L.E.* 30)

She is lethal to her lovers—'. . . las tijeras . . . tres gotas de luz fría . . .'—and beautiful, but inanimate and vaguely threatening.

The second lady (*L.E.* 32) is more obviously a power of the dark. She is sinister in her hardness, 'inexorable rompehielos', and globe-trotting in her career, moving from Costa Rica to the Himalayas and to Africa, changing male and female lovers, and coming to rest at the age of forty-five, specifically at 'Proserpina Court, int. 2, Bombay', where she practises witchcraft with her Parsi lover. She is an emanation of the spirit of evil in female form, world-pervading, fickle, and perverse, and in her presence even the fire-worshipping Parsi turns heretic. The precision of the physical description, and the exact age and address at once make the suggestion of witchcraft more menacing, and add to the irony of tone. In both of these 'Golden Lotuses' poems it is this irony which preserves the balance between the cosmic and religious connotations of the title, and the underworld tinges of meaning which the poems convey. The combination of both elements, the sublime and the evil, light and dark, is, of course, in keeping with the non-diverse outlook of Indian myth. Technically speaking, these elements are synthesized in the poems through the poet's ironic tone which *per se* admits of a polyvalent vision of the poem's subject.

Irony is tinged, perhaps even replaced, by nostalgia in 'Golden Lotuses' (3) (*L.E.* 34). The lady here lives in a large, uncared-for house, with empty rooms and portraits of forgotten celebrities. Her existence and her surroundings would seem forgotten by the world, but she gives life to the house as the wind gives life to her:

> La casa está habitada por una mujer rubia.
> La mujer está habitada por el viento.
>
> (*L.E.* 34)

The introduction of the wind adds the element of ambiguity which is a less obvious but effective hinge between title and subject. A woman inhabited by the wind might be insubstantial, ghostlike, a nothing person whom existence has abandoned. Yet as Quetzal-coatl is also the god of wind because it was wind which breathed life into the sun,[35] so the wind is also a life-force in the creation myth which Zimmer relates. The renewal of the universe at the start of each *kalpa* or Brahman-day is a slow progression of creation as Vishnu, the Highest Being, in the form of water, visualizes the form of the universe in its five elements:

> Vishnu, having entered the water, gently stirred it. Waves rippled. As they followed each other, there was formed among them a tiny cleft. This cleft was space or ether, invisible, intangible, the most subtle of the five elements; carrier of the invisible, intangible sense-quality of sound. Space resounded, and from the sound arose the second element, air, in the form of a wind.[36]

The power of the wind creates friction and then fire, until finally comes the lotus flower with Brahma in its centre, and the cycle is in process again. Thus wind is universally a sign of life and energy, and the image of the empty house and faded celebrities becomes an ambiguous one, as the woman in whom the wind dwells becomes herself a double symbol, perhaps lifeless, perhaps regenerative, an empty existence, or an instrument in the cycle of death and rebirth.

The three poems, though seemingly slight, when examined as a group, show an intuition of the female principle in the universe completely in keeping with Hindu traditions. The serpentine quality of the first lady recalls Melusina, a loving wife and mother until her scales were seen, and Eve, with their charms fatal for the men whom they love. The same intuition of dangerous powers is incarnate in Kali dancing on the prostrate Shiva. The monthly

cycle of womanhood is a sign of fertility, but also of the rituals of
witchcraft dependent on the moon, symbol of chastity. The paradoxes are unceasing, but taken all together they create woman, the
manifestation of the Earth Mother, the cosmic lotus—source of
energy, rebirth, and mystery.

'Viento entero' (*L.E.* 101–8) merits much attention, but at a
later point in this study.[37] It contains only one passage in which
the old myths are drawn on as analogies to the human situation,
and the allusion is of the simplest. Shiva and his consort Parvati
(one of the names given to her when not in her Kali manifestation)
represent the sacred union of the Two-in-One, the 'first and
primal unfolding of the neuter Brahman into the opposites of the
male and female principles'.[38] As such they represent perfect
harmony, and can never be in discord. They are complementary to
each other and their natures are inseparable. One of their favourite
resorts is Mount Kailasa, which is among the first creations of
Brahma, 'el pico del mundo'. Zimmer describes Kailasa as 'the
mountain of the heart, wherein the fire of life, the energy of
the creator, is quick with the ardor of its eternal source and at
the same instant throbbing with the pulse of time'.[39] In the
union there of Shiva and Parvati 'Eternity and Life [are] one
and the same'.[40]

In 'Viento entero' Paz creates a complex web of themes behind
which the essence of passion hangs like a backdrop, at once in and
out of time. The act of love is an intense consummation of the
moment, but also a rite of passage which transcends time in a
wider consciousness of oneness with the essential harmony of the
universe. Love is a Janus figure, looking towards the present
moment, lived at its fullest, and looking out of time, into an eternal
world of myth:

> El presente es perpetuo
> En el pico del mundo se acarician
> Shiva y Parvati
> Cada caricia dura un siglo
> Para el dios y para el hombre
> Un mismo tiempo
> Un mismo despeñarse . . .
>
> (*L.E.* 107)

Man and woman become one with Shiva and Parvati in an embrace
which ends only to begin again in a never-ending circle of love and

fulfilment, both affirming the present and immortalizing it. The symbolism of the love of the divine couple implies the resolution of opposites, or to use Paz's analogy the harmonizing of all rhythms in 'Un latido idéntico'.

The same comparison is drawn in 'Domingo en la isla de Elefanta' (*L.E.* 128–9), though in this poem Paz makes more assertive his personal interpretation of the myth and the existential meaning of his transcendence of normal consciousness. The Island of Elephanta is on the western coast of India near Bombay, and a temple to Shiva was built in its caves during the eighth century A.D.[41] The sculptures in these caves are among the best examples of Indian art, though they were defaced by over-zealous Moslems and Portuguese Christians.[42] The central shrine contains a colossal bust of Shiva as the 'Great Lord', a three-headed image twenty-three feet high. Zimmer interprets this statue as follows:

The head at the beholder's left is male, that at the right female, while in the center is the visage of the world-supporting, transcendent, un-differentiated essence of the creative void. The devotee is to think of the divine generative principle as manifest, left and right, in the comple-mentary poles of the male and the female, the world-mothering prin-ciple residing in the latter; and in the former, in the aspect of anger, the force of destruction.[43]

On the panel to the right of the Great God is the wedding scene of Shiva and Parvati, a visual objectification, as it were, of the ideology synthesized in the Shiva Mahesvara, the three-headed figure, or as Zimmer continues, 'a reaffirmation of the male–female polarity'. The panel on the left shows the androgynous Shiva, the Shiva Ardhanari, another manifestation of the same principle.

Paz's poem opens with an attack on despoilers, both the crowds who leave behind them 'un *picnic* de basura', and the 'mutiladores de estatuas'. All of them he consigns to a hundred reincarnations in a dunghill. Then he invokes Shiva and Parvati as symbols of all the divine potential within man himself:

> Shiva y Parvati:
> Los adoramos
> No como a dioses,
> Como a imágenes
> De la divinidad de los hombres.
> (*L.E.* 128)

The love relationship is for him a source of movement from one level of consciousness to a higher level, but man contains within himself the seeds of all possible greatness:

> Ustedes son lo que el hombre hace y no es,
> Lo que el hombre ha de ser
> Cuando pague la condena del quehacer.
>
> (*L.E.* 128)

The poet turns to describe the sculptures themselves, and these lead him out to the emanations of the same principle of cosmic harmony in Nature:

> El mar palpita bajo el sol:
> Son los gruesos labios de Shiva que sonríe;
> El mar es una larga llamarada:
> Son los pasos de Parvati sobre las aguas.
>
> (*L.E.* 129)

This principle has shown itself to him in terms of human beings and human existence also:

> Shiva y Parvati:
>   La mujer que es mi mujer
> Y yo,
>   Nada les pedimos, nada
> Que sea del otro mundo:
>   Sólo
> La luz sobre el mar,
> La luz descalza sobre el mar y la tierra dormidos.
>
> (*L.E.* 129)

In this very specific merging of his own beliefs with age-old myths, Paz shows in the most obvious way both the essential structure of his thought and his transposition of this into the mythic mode. There is available to human beings an awakening on a higher level in which the principles of cosmic harmony can be perceived by those who will see them. Love is the most available path to transcendence of selfhood, and man, while not committed to any religious creed, can grasp thereby the eternal truths which all mythologies and religions have formulated. The other shore can be reached, even though the other world is denied. The threshold of man's consciousness can be raised after initiation—the giving of oneself in love, or some parallel process—yet man's existence is for

Paz very much a question of this earth, with all the glorious possibilities and inevitable ending of this life.

In *Ladera Este* there are four poems in particular which depend upon the philosophies lying behind the Indian mythological traditions. They show Paz's capacity to deal with metaphysical concepts on an extremely high intellectual level while still adapting them to the structure of his own metaphysics. At the same time he welds them into poems which could never be criticized as 'intellectual', as he never fails to handle even the most complex ideas with the intuition and the verbal exactitude which the word 'poetry' implies. This is to say that Paz as a thinker is fully capable of handling the concepts with which he deals; Paz as a poet extracts from them the essence which illuminates all great philosophy.

'Sunyata' (*L.E.* 97) takes the reader into the heart of Mahayana Buddhism and its concept of the void. The poem presents a moment when time seems suspended—a relatively simple concept yet with profound implications. The day is like a tree, or perhaps there is also a tree; in any case these images are superimposed in the burning heat, making together a 'Presencia que se consume / En una gloria sin sustancia'. Matter and time are moving into a nothingness, where such terms lose their meaning. The hours fall away like leaves from the tree, till what is left is 'un tallo de vibraciones / Que se disipan'. When negation of time, natural beauty, and Being itself are no more than 'tantas / Beatitudes indiferentes', the negation of all things produces its own negation, thus avoiding all dialectic, and the same day is reborn, the same sun felt on the eyelids, and the day and the tree exist again.

Paz provides a note which is succinct and clear:

... todo es relativo e impermanente, sin excluir a la afirmación sobre la relatividad e impermanencia del mundo. La proposición que niega la realidad también se disuelve y así la negación del mundo por la crítica es asimismo su recuperación ... (*L.E.* 180)

A little more exposition of the ideas expressed will not, perhaps, be amiss, since the relationship of being and nothingness in a non-dualistic vision is so clearly allied to the union of opposites throughout Paz's poetry.

Mahayana Buddhism, the final Buddhist teaching of 'The Great Ferry-boat' as opposed to the Hinayana ('The Little Ferry-boat') philosophy, was spread, if not formulated, by Nagarjuna[44] in the second or third century A.D. Nagarjuna's *Madhyamika Sastra* (*The Guide-book of the School of the Middle Way*) presents the traditional concepts of the mystery of enlightenment of the schools of India, emphasizing, for example, the existence of two truths, one relative and conditional, the other absolute and transcendent, of which nothing can be preached in words. The innovation of Nagarjuna was his approach to the concept of *sunyata*, 'the Void': 'It cannot be called void or not void; or both or neither, but in order to indicate it, it is called The Void.'[45] The non-duality of *samsara*, the endless round of being, and *nirvana*, release or nothingness, was known and sung in other branches of Indian religious thought (the Vedanta Gitas, for instance), but 'in this Buddhist formula, one word, *sunyata*, bears the entire message, and simultaneously projects the mind beyond any attempt to conceive of a synthesis'.[46] It does indeed mark a middle way, that between negation and affirmation, and between *nirvana* and *samsara* which become as one, void. Zimmer quotes the *Samyutta-Nikaya* thus:

> That things have being, O Kaccana, constitutes one extreme of doctrine; that things have no being is the other extreme. These extremes, O Kaccana, have been avoided by the Tathagata, and it is a middle doctrine that he teaches.[47]

The mind, through the concept of *sunyata*, rises beyond its natural tendency to confront one thing with its opposite, or to create antitheses. *Sunyata* invalidates paradox.

Thus in Paz's 'sunyata' the passing of the hours and the falling of the leaves are part of the illusion of *samsara*; the 'beatitudes indiferentes' are an equally illusory *nirvana*. *Sunyata* lies beyond both, includes them and annuls them. Strictly speaking, of course, to call a poem 'Sunyata' is to undo the very concept itself, since a poem, whatever it expresses, exists in its own right as a verbal form. However, approached not as a pure expression of Buddhist philosophy, but as the personal system of interrogation of the world which it is, both in itself and as part of Paz's *œuvre*, 'Sunyata' is a perfectly expressed, perfectly balanced entity. The double images of day and tree, with the heat of the sun as a background motif ('yesca', 'calcinado', 'vibraciones', 'brasa'), move together through the death and rebirth process to the final synthesis of the last line:

El día   El árbol

In this unpunctuated balance, which is also the essence of the whole poem, Olson's definition seems particularly accurate: 'Form is never more than an extension of content.'[48]

'Maithuna' (*L.E.* 116-21) is a ten-sectioned rhapsody to erotic passion, mounting to a climax which must be one of the most amazing *tours de force* of love-poetry in any language. Love of the mind, yes, but more specifically love of the body, the human equivalent of the blending of opposites in single union, the return to the Two-in-One. Here Paz's intuition again merges with the philosophies of India, 'maithuna' (sexual intercourse) being one of the 'five forbidden things' which Tantra sanctifies in its insistence on the holiness and purity of all manifestations of life.[49] The others are wine (*madya*), meat (*mamsa*), fish (*matsya*), and parched grain (*mudra*), and Tantric rites use these earlier taboos as holy fare to demonstrate the non-dualistic realization of the world as one, sanctified and unsullied. Here the Tantric development of Hindu thought met with the Mahayana vision of non-differentiation. In Mahayana Buddhism concentrated meditation on an icon is seen as a way to lead the mind to the source of inspiration as it is manifested in the icon, and thence to the void. The Mahayana equivalent of *maithuna* is *mahasukha*, 'the Great Delight', and the icons symbolizing this show the divine male and female (the Tibetan *Yab-Yum*) making love.[50] Contemplation of the ritual sexual act leads the devotee through an awareness of both principles, male and female, alternately activating and receiving, into what Zimmer calls 'the mystery of the cosmogonic manifestation of compassion'. The right understanding of *sunyata* guides the believer into the awareness that both principles are functions of reality of equal rank. As in the principle of *samsara* and *nirvana*, enlightenment shows that the apparent difference, here between male and female, is non-existent.

So closely does the philosophic system behind *maithuna* and *mahasukha* parallel the structure of Paz's intuitive vision of love from his earliest poems to the latest, 'Blanco', that Zimmer's description of the Great Delight warrants quotation in full:

In the sexual act it is possible to recognize a pre-eminent rendition and profound human experience of the metaphysical mystery of the nondual entity which is made manifest as two. The embrace of the male and female principles, and their delight thereby, denote their intrinsic unity, their metaphysical identity. Regarded from the standpoint of logic in the world of space and time, the male and female are two. But in their intuition of their identity (which is the seed of love) the thought of twoness is transcended, while from the mystery of their physical union (their enactment and experience in time of their real and secret nonduality) a new being is produced—as though the corporeal imitation of the transcorporeal, nondual truth had magically touched the inexhaustible spring from which the phenomena of the cosmos arise. Through the sexual act, that is to say, creatures of the visible world actually come into touch, in experience, with the metaphysical sphere of the nondual source. The latter is not absolutely apart and unrelated. It is, rather, their own very essence, which they experience in every impulse of compassion—but supremely in that supreme human realization of compassion which is known in the enactment of the mystery play of the sexes.[51]

Such a vision lends shape to 'Maithuna'. The ten sections are all complete in themselves, in fact the second appears alone in the *Discos visuales*,[52] and the unity of the whole poem is one of situation and vision. The length of the sections varies and is inessential to the poem as a whole; what the eye perceives is a growth in the length of the line as it moves towards the middle of the poem, and a consequent shortening, palindrome-fashion, from the middle to the end, with the laconic purity of the final section. The poem's imagery follows a similar trajectory, from initial economy to the richness of section six, with its fantasy of the long hair like a tongue on the woman's back, the tongue image leading to that of language, thence to writing:

> Cabellera
> Lengua de látigos
> Lenguajes
> Sobre tu espalda desatados
> Entrelazados
> Sobre tus senos
> Escritura que te escribe
> Con letras aguijones
> Te niega
> Con signos tizones
> Vestidura que te desviste
> Escritura que te viste de adivinanzas
> Escritura en la que me entierro . . .
> (*L.E.* 119)

Then comes a moving back in section seven to economy of image, based here on Li-Po, the haiku poet who inspired many of the works of Juan José Tablada, and finally the verbal virtuosity of the closing sections.

The brilliance of the last section, which draws analogies from Nature, but depends entirely for its effect on language, on poetic technique in fact, draws the reader into the other dimension of transcendence for which Paz struggles—the emergence of the poem as a verbal structure from the web of emotions and language which are the raw material of every man, but which only a few can fashion so that sign and significance become one and the same. In the supreme moment of transcendence, passion and language blend as the threshold of consciousness expands, and the vision given by sexual union becomes one with the poem:

> Y nueva nubemente sube
> Savia
>   (Salvia te llamo
> Llama)
>   El tallo
> Estalla
>   (Llueve
> Nieve ardiente)
>   Mi lengua está
> Allá
>   (En la nieve se quema
> Tu rosa)
>   Está
> Ya
>   (Sello tu sexo)
>   El alba
> Salva

(L.E. 121)

'Lectura de John Cage' (*L.E.* 80–4) is Paz's response to the aesthetic of Cage in general, and in particular to Cage's two volumes of writings and lectures, *Silence* (Middletown, Conn., 1961) and *A Year from Monday* (Middletown, Conn., 1967). Paradoxically, Cage, though originally a composer, seems to have more influence in the literary world than in the musical, where he arouses much hostile resistance. For many poets, and also painters, however, he is the new prophet, the catalyst of the spirit of experimentation and anti-art which has been somewhat in abeyance since the days of Dada. Cage is very close to the Japanese tradition of Zen Buddhism in his philosophy, and in many ways he has seemed to Paz a kindred spirit; though Paz, as noted earlier, sees concordances between his own thought and Oriental traditions without adopting them to his own experience as Cage tries to do.

The nexus of Cage's aesthetics, as his writings show, is the avoidance of any polar situation. The teachings of Zen have led Cage to an 'identification with what is here and now',[53] an identification complete enough to erase the oppositions which seem to divide subject from object, for instance, art from life, or music from silence. Cage thus combines philosophy and aesthetics (probably indivisible in his mind) with the non-duality emphasized in Eastern systems of thought, and it is here that he echoes the intuitive responses of Paz to life and the universe.

In his desire to eliminate dialectic, Cage blurs the line normally drawn between music and noise and that between music and silence. Furthermore, he quotes Schoenberg[54] to make the point that unmaking is a crucial part of the process of making, a paradox extended by Paz in his opening: 'Leído / Desleído . . .' One of Cage's favourite stories concerns his attempt to find silence, which he maintains does not exist outside the mind, by entering an anechoic chamber at Harvard:

. . . in that silent room, I heard two sounds, one high and one low. Afterwards I asked the engineer in charge why, if the room was silent, I had heard two sounds. He said, 'Describe them.' I did. He said, 'The high one was your nervous system in operation. The low one was your blood in circulation.'[55]

So for Cage there is no escape from sound, and thus from music; sound is in the nature of life itself. This is the point to which Paz moves with his exploration of synaesthesia, and his parallels between apparent dichotomies of music and silence, and of architecture and space. Cage says that 'there is no such thing as an empty space or an empty time'.[56] Paz's conclusion is the same: silence, like space, is an unattainable ideal which we can know only in terms of what it is not—music or architecture. We cannot make silence, says Cage, and Paz:

> No hay silencio
> Salvo en la mente.
> El silencio es una idea,
> La idea fija de la música.
> (*L.E.* 81)

What we have is music, 'sonidos caminando sobre el silencio', and life, not some artificial division called 'art', but a synthesis in which dichotomies evaporate:

> Silencio es música
> > Música no es silencio.
> Nirvana es Samsara
> > Samsara no es Nirvana.
> > > *(L.E.* 81)

We know silence only in terms of music, likewise we know release (*nirvana*) only in terms of the daily stuff of life (*samsara*), yet the differences are unreal, as wisdom is a passing through knowledge to an awareness of ignorance:

> El saber no es saber:
> > Recobrar la ignorancia,
> Saber del saber.
> > > *(L.E.* 81)

What Cage does is precisely this: by coming between ourselves and our dogmatism he shows the way to recovery of ignorance. Music in his hands is a bridge between silence and meaning:

> > Silencio no tiene sentido
> > Sentido no tiene silencio.
> Sin ser oída
> > La música se desliza entre ambos.
> > > *(L.E.* 82)

It is a bridge also between something (*samsara*) and nothing (*nirvana*), between the poet's body and his wife's body—'(*A cable of sound*)'—it is communication, it is real. Music, or Cage through music, shows how to accept contraries and harmonize them, not to choose:

> *(The situation must be Yes-and-No*
> > *Not either-or)* ·
> > > *(L.E.* 83) ·

Cage teaches a non-commitment which is a total acceptance, a concordance of opposites: silence and music, art and life, snow and sun. 'Committed to the nothing-in-between', which is total unity, he speaks, and all things meet, not in silence, but in the word which he creates. Cage himself provides a quotation from Meister Eckhart which illuminates his own transcendence of paradox.

Talking of something and nothing, and how they need each other, he quotes these words from the Christian mystic: 'Earth [that is any something] has no escape from heaven [that is nothing]: flee she up or flee she down heaven still invades her, energizing her, fructifying her, whether for her weal or her woe.'[57]

To readers of Paz, the ultimate resolution of sound and meaning, and of art and life, is the poem on the page. And one of Cage's comments is particularly apposite to the new direction of Paz's poetry in the last fifteen years or so, with its careful typographical layout so obviously making space on the page and time in the reading into prime elements of its form. In the foreword to *Silence* Cage says: 'As I see it, poetry is not prose simply because poetry is in one way or another formalized. It is not poetry by reason of its content or its ambiguity, but by reason of its allowing musical elements (time, sound) to be introduced into the world of words.' So in its very technique the poem is a concordance of sound and sense, of sound and silence, and of the signs with the blank page on which they come to lie. Paz's awareness of the poem in a time–space dimension becomes more apparent in 'Blanco', but all these preoccupations with art as catalyst and synthesis are as obvious in 'Lectura de John Cage' as they are in the writings of Cage himself.

'Vrindaban' (*L.E.* 57–63) recalls 'Solo a dos voces' in its fusion of the act of composition with metaphysical considerations, but it is unique both in its occasion and in its resolution. Like so many other poems it shows Paz as consummate technician and profound human being: the delicacy of its fabric makes more amazing the forcefulness of its expression. The place of the title recalls one of the most celebrated events in Hindu mythology, Vishnu's coming to earth in his most popular incarnation, Krishna.[58] Krishna and his half-brother Balarama were born to a human mother, and Krishna's first mission was to overcome the demon Kalanemi, at that moment incarnate as Kamsa. The community into which Krishna was born, unaware of his divinity, moved for safety to Vrindavan on the banks of the sacred river Yamuna, and across from Kamsa's city, Mathura. The early life of Krishna, archetype of the divine child, provides some of the favourite themes of Hindu mythology. It was at Vrindavan that Krishna fought and vanquished the serpent king Kaliya, who was then banished. The point of interest here to Occidental minds is that the demon is not killed, since he too is a manifestation of God's essence, though of its darker side, and that the counterplay between productive and destructive energies may be corrected, but never disrupted.

In this spot, sacred to Hindu religious philosophy, the poet faces himself, exploring his limitations and his potential as man and as poet. He writes at night, aware of the living, shifting quality of the atmosphere surrounding him, and aware as he writes of the impossibility of fixing this moving reality upon the page before him:

> (Todo está y no está
> Todo calladamente se desmorona
> Sobre la página) . . .
>
> (*L.E.* 57)

He considers the duality of the human being: on the physical level he was being driven home a little while before through silent streets, while on the spiritual plane his mind was fusing with the immensity of the natural and phenomenal world around him:

> Yo era un árbol y hablaba
> Estaba cubierto de hojas y ojos
> Yo era el murmullo que avanza
> El enjambre de imágenes . . .
>
> (*L.E.* 57)

Now the paradox is born in on him as he draws signs on paper in an attempt to represent what he has felt:

> (Ahora trazo unos cuantos signos
> Crispados
> Negro sobre blanco
> Diminuto jardín de letras
> A la luz de una lámpara plantado) . . .
>
> (*L.E.* 57–8)

His thoughts have brought him face to face with words, commonplaces, trite, facile expressions, and with his own beliefs, which he suspends—'(Aquí intervienen los puntos / Suspensivos)'—to recall the evidence of his eyes.

He sees the teeming life of an Indian town with the squalor of its beggars, the almost corporeal smells of sandalwood, jasmine, and decay; the universe, like this microcosm, is a fever of changing forms and passing time, never the same, but all reflecting some single essence, some wider unity:

> Cola de pavo real el universo entero
> Miríades de ojos

En otros ojos reflejados
Modulaciones reverberaciones de un ojo único
Un solitario sol . . .

(*L.E.* 59)

Before his eyes the whole scene, shimmering in the sun, blends
from individual forms to a blur of colour and a single blazing light.
In his ears, the sounds of Nature and of men crystallize in the
voice rising from the temple:

La voz humana
Luna en celo por el mediodía
Queja del alma que se desencarna . . .

(*L.E.* 60)

The voice seeking to be heard leads in transition to the lamp in
whose light the poet struggles towards expression:

(Escribo sin conocer el desenlace
De lo que escribo
                    Busco entre líneas
Mi imagen es la lámpara
                              Encendida
En mitad de la noche) . . .

(*L.E.* 60)

His search for release in words alternates with the image of a
Hindu ascetic whose choice has been withdrawal from the human
sphere to some reality incommunicable to others. Paz first treats
this figure ambivalently, as though this refusal to reach out to other
human beings could cloak enlightenment or fraud:

Saltimbanqui
Mono de lo Absoluto . . .

(*L.E.* 80)

His denial of the world has taken him to some other shore: '¿A qué
existencia a la intemperie de qué mundos / En qué tiempo?' Here
the use of the word 'orilla' has a double impact. In the context of
Indian philosophy the 'Wisdom of the Other Shore' is the enlightenment towards which all strive. In Mahayana Buddhism it is
the Buddhahood available to all who entrust themselves to the
Great Ferry-boat. Among the strangest of Buddhist texts are those
named *Prajna-paramita* ('The Wisdom [*prajna*] Gone to the Other
Shore [*paramita*]'), described by Zimmer as 'a series of the most

curious dialogues, conducted in a sort of conversation-circle of Buddhas and Bodhisattvas . . . [who] entertain themselves with enigmatical statements of the unstatable truth'.[59] So for the believer the other shore is part of the metaphor of the ferry-boat, and its attainment is the release of *sunyata*, beyond all polarities. Yet this concept of reaching another shore, that is, another level of consciousness, has always existed in Paz's poetry, and 'la orilla' is a part of his personal vocabulary,[60] with its connotations of initiation and emergence. For instance, in 'Arcos' (*Lib.* 35–6) of 1947, the image of a river appears into which the poet must step 'sin detenerme en una orilla', in order to gain the new awareness. Other echoes are therefore aroused in the reader's memory by the image of the holy man removed to some far region of consciousness.

The poet turns into his writing again, memory forcing him on, and bringing back to his mind the puzzling figure of the old man, 'Santo pícaro santo'. The poet is haunted by this other-worldliness and its possibilities:

> Arrobos del hambre o de la droga
> Tal vez vio a Krishna
> > Árbol azul[61] y centelleante . . .
> > > (*L.E.* 61)

Now as the poet returns to the opening parallel of his body moving in the car and his thoughts roaming, a synthesis begins to take place. The physical and the spiritual blend, and the ambivalence of the holy man disappears, or ceases to matter:

> (Ido ido
> Santo payaso santo mendigo rey maldito
> Es lo mismo
> > Siempre lo mismo
> > > En lo mismo
> Es ser siempre en sí mismo
> > > Encerrado
> En lo mismo
> > En sí mismo cerrado
> Ídolo podrido)
> > > (*L.E.* 62)

A contrast is established, however, between the impassive 'other shore' of the old man and the 'hora inestable' in which the poet moves through time and space, both mentally and physically. He accepts for himself a transcendence which is not a release from the things of the world but is none the less valid for him:

> Los absolutos las eternidades
> Y sus aledaños
>   No son mi tema
> Tengo hambre de vida y también de morir
> Sé lo que creo y lo escribo . . .
>   (*L.E.* 62)

The self must look inward, but it must re-emerge, may withdraw into memory, but must return in

>   El acto
>   El movimiento en que se esculpe
>   Y se deshace el ser entero . . .
>   (*L.E.* 62)

He acknowledges his existence in time—'Soy una historia / Una memoria que se inventa'—but for him there is the poem, the meaning behind the signs which he makes on the paper, the lamp in the darkness:

> Hablo siempre contigo Hablas siempre conmigo
> A oscuras voy y planto signos . . .
>   (*L.E.* 63)

Poetry is his way to the other shore, his rebirth after withdrawal. The completed form of the poem on the page is his own release from differentiation, and from the diversity of the forms and words which obscures man's vision of the oneness of being.

Paz himself provides an apposite ending for this attempt to discover an experiential and a technical structure as constants in his poetry. 'Cuento de dos jardines' (*L.E.* 130–41) pulls together the threads of the mythic mode as it describes two gardens paramount and reiterative in Paz's life pattern:

>   Un día
>   Como si regresara
>   No a mi casa:
>   Al comienzo del Comienzo . . .
>   (*L.E.* 133)

The section of *Ladera Este* in which this poem appears is called 'Hacia el comienzo', and 'Cuento de dos jardines' provides the key to this title by elaborating the idea of a return to a timeless beginning, which is so much the pattern of mythic thought, with, of course, its parallels in Freudian and Jungian psycho-analysis.[62]

The two gardens which Paz recalls are first that of his childhood in Mixcoac, and then the Indian garden where he remarried, both representing moments of expanding consciousness in his life. The opening lines establish the mythic properties which a house and a garden may have, mythic in the sense that they can take us into a dimension beyond the mere space they enclose, and into a time which is beyond human time, in exactly the same way that all mythologies take man back to an ideal time and space which re-enact the 'Great Time, the holy time of the beginnings', *illud tempus*.[63] Gardens, for the poet, represent moments of escape from profane time, moments so intense, however, that they can be held only as the new awareness dawns, and must then return to memory as daily life goes on:

> Sus apariciones
> Abren en el espacio
> Otro espacio,
> Otro tiempo en el tiempo.
> Sus eclipses
> No son abdicaciones:
> Nos quemaría
> La vivacidad de uno de esos instantes
> Si durase otro instante.

(*L.E.* 130)

Over the childhood garden, 'un cuerpo / Cubierto de heridas', looms the presence of the fig-tree, 'la Madre, / la Diosa',[64] and in the garden he has his first intimation of death:

> El mundo se entreabrió:
> Yo creí que había visto a la muerte
> Al ver
> La otra cara del ser,
> La vacía:
> El fijo resplandor sin atributos.

(*L.E.* 132)

The atmosphere of Mexico which the garden evokes recalls earlier poems, though with the great stylistic differences mentioned earlier:

> México: sobre la piedra ensangrentada
> Danza el agua.

Meses de espejos.
El hormiguero,
Sus ritos subterráneos . . .
(*L.E.* 132)

One senses a lonely childhood filled with almost visionary intuitions:

Sed, tedio, tolvaneras:
Impalpables epifanías de viento.
Los pinos me enseñaron a hablar solo.
En aquel jardín aprendí a despedirme.
(*L.E.* 133)

The next garden is the return 'al comienzo del Comienzo', full of light, water, and colour, and overshadowed by the giant *nim* tree, 'grande como el monumento de la paciencia', yet aware of its role in the wider scheme of things. In the shade of this (to him) symbolic tree new truths are learned, and a new maturity gained:

Supe que estaba vivo,
Supe que morir es ensancharse,
Negarse es crecer.
Entre gula y soberbia,
Codicia de vida
O fascinación por la muerte,
La vía de en medio.
En la fraternidad de los árboles
Aprendí a reconciliarme,
No conmigo:
Con lo que me levanta y me sostiene y me deja caer.
(*L.E.* 135)

It is now, in the teeming life of India, that the poet meets the woman with whom he experiences new truths and new concordances:

Un jardín no es un lugar:
Es un tránsito,
Una pasión:
No sabemos hacia donde vamos,
Transcurrir es suficiente,
Transcurrir es quedarse.
(*L.E.* 137)

The poem evolves through fairytale (the story of Almendrita), myth (*Yakshi*, or dryad), metaphor, descriptions of nature and of birds, all adding up to a magical atmosphere of unlimited horizons:

> Geometrías aéreas,
> Veloces constelaciones en pleno día.
> (*L.E.* 139)

Then it reaches the final situation, the sea journey from Bombay to the Canaries which leaves behind the garden, except in so far as its symbolism is carried within:

> El jardín se ha quedado atrás.
> ¿Atrás o adelante?
> No hay más jardines que los que llevamos dentro.
> (*L.E.* 139)

At the close of the poem the metaphor of the other shore reappears, crystallized in a statement of transcendence, but in human terms, through passion:

> Pasión es tránsito:
> La otra orilla está aquí,
> Luz en el aire sin orillas:
> *Prainaparamita*
> Nuestra Señora de la Otra Orilla,
> Tu misma,
> La muchacha del cuento
> La alumna del jardín.
> (*L.E.* 139–140)

What enlightenment he will know will be here, in and through love, and a remarkable personification occurs in these lines where the fairy-tale world of Alemendrita (Thumbelina) and the real world of the girl in the garden blend into the most transcendental female figure in Mahayana Buddhism, Prajna-Paramita, the female aspect of the Universal Buddha, with overtones of Christian idealism carried by the phrase 'Nuestra Señora'. Zimmer explains how the ancient pattern of the goddess Lotus, Mother Earth, Magna Mater, 'procreative energy and fortune on the physical plane', became transfigured under the influence of mature Buddhist and late Hindu conceptions into 'the highest representative of world-transcending wakefulness, the most spiritual feminine symbol in . . . the East'. Prajna-Paramita, the 'Wisdom of the Other Shore', the Buddhist version of Sophia, enlightening knowledge, is the personified truth of the Buddhist law, 'the adamantine, indestructible, secret nature of all and everything, itself devoid of all limiting, differentiating characteristics'.[65]

Love of and in the woman he has found is, in the structure of Paz's vision, the moment of encounter with eternal truth. Here he finds the wisdom to which Nagarjuna and Dharmakirti pointed the way, here he finds *sunyata*, moment of undifferentiated vision. When he returns, in conclusion, to the physical universe around him, 'Sombras girando / Sobre un charco de luz. / Mergos y ¿peces?', it is to find all transfigured in the light of new vision:

> Se absima
> El jardín en una identidad
> > Sin nombre
> Ni sustancia.
> > Los signos se borran: yo miro la claridad.
> > > > (*L.E.* 141)

There is still much ground to cover in order to establish in adequate terms the architecture of Paz's poetic world. Paz's use of myth is the most obvious outer cover for the inner structure. He has intuited what structural anthropologists such as Lévi-Strauss have demonstrated, namely that myths widely divergent in time and space can be reduced to their component parts ('mythemes', in Lévi-Strauss's terms),[66] and that the relationship between these parts is systematic and the same. But Paz has gone further, and has transformed these myths by his ability to re-enact in them his own spiritual pilgrimage. He has grasped the essential analogy between the mythic trajectory as it is variously expressed by different mentalities and at different times, and the changing states of perception from which his poetry is drawn. Hence the ease with which his poetry adopts the 'mythic mode', using familiar traditions whose pattern underscores the coherence of his poetic world.

The mythic mode allows Paz's private cosmogony to turn most readily out to the world of creeds and races. For this reason it has appeared first in this study, as the least hermetic and most easily explored of the modes of his expression. It shows the richness of Paz's mind, his deep identification with his country, and also his wide experience of other systems and philosophies. It allows him to clothe his epistemological anxieties in comfortingly familiar garb, so that his individual divergencies and assertions are less startling, as they adhere to recognizable forms of thought. Other modes will take us more directly to the core of the universe built by Paz's poetic imagination, but the richness of allusion and drama evoked by the myths of East and West provides its own enchantment. It adds a very special dimension to the world of Paz's work.

II

THE SURREALIST MODE

THERE is a definite period in Octavio Paz's career when his poetry may be considered as set in a surrealist mode. Chronological precision is impossible when dealing with the intangibilities of a creative psyche, and traces of a predisposition to a surrealist outlook appear early. Yet the three collections in which this mode is most apparent are those which contain Paz's writing of the 50s: *¿Aguila o sol?*, the prose poems of 1949–50 (*Lib.* 145–207), *La estación violenta*, which appeared in 1957 and contains major works from 1948–57 (*Lib.* 209–54), and *Salamandra*, whose poems are from 1958 to 1961 and which appeared in 1969 in its second edition. (The first edition dates from 1962.) Paz was closely associated with the surrealist group in Paris when André Breton returned there after the Second World War, and there is obviously a correspondence between his own years in Paris and his change in literary style. Yet Paz never gave up his poetic independence to become a committed member of this group, and so did not assume the title of surrealist proper. It is more accurate to say that he found in the ideas and practices of the Surrealists affinities with his spiritual state and his linguistic theories at that time. The Surrealists' exploration of the whole self by taking into account the individual's dream and fantasy worlds as well as his conscious level of existence tends towards a unitive view of the psyche which echoes in all Paz's writings in one form or another. Again, the deliberate dislocation of the image in order to shock the recipient into a new vision is particularly apt for the expression of a state of mind which is 'out of joint' with itself and its universe. This is, in fact, the prevailing mood of *Salamandra*, and is implicit in the linguistic and imagistic struggles of *¿Aguila o sol?* In terms of the mythic cycle which I see as the structure basic to Paz's work, the anguished rites of initiation preceding spiritual rebirth gain in poignancy when set in a mode which explores the underside of the mind as an indispensable complement to the conscious.

Paz's prose writings make constant reference to the Surrealists, Breton and Peret, for instance, as well as to writers considered precursors of the movement, Lautréamont and Apollinaire.[1] Apollinaire was the first to coin the term 'surréalisme', when in 1917 in a programme note to the Satie–Massine–Picasso ballet *Parade*, produced by Diaghilev, he called this unique collaboration a kind of 'surréalisme'.[2] André Breton seized upon the new term as applicable to his own vision of art a few years later, though he hesitated between this and Gérard de Nerval's 'supernaturalisme', feeling that: 'Il semble, en effet, que Nerval posséda à merveille *l'esprit* dont nous nous réclamons, Apollinaire n'ayant possédé, par contre, que *la lettre*, encore imparfaite, du surréalisme et s'étant montré impuissant à en donner un aperçu théorique qui nous retienne.'[3]

Breton himself is quite explicit in his description of this new spirit which was to combine the world of reality with the dream world 'en une sorte de réalité absolue, de *surréalité*, si l'on peut ainsi dire'.[4] Breton's knowledge of Freudian theories and his application of these in his work in neuro-psychiatric centres during the First World War are apparent in his formal definition of the term in the 1924 *Manifeste*:

SURRÉALISME, n. m. Automatisme psychique pur par lequel on se propose d'exprimer, soit verbalement, soit par écrit, soit de toute autre manière, le fonctionnement réel de la pensée. Dictée de la pensée, en l'absence de tout contrôle exercé par la raison, en dehors de toute préoccupation esthétique ou morale.

ENCYCL. *Philos.* Le surréalisme repose sur la croyance à la réalité supérieure de certaines formes d'associations négligées jusqu'à lui, à la toutepuissance du rêve, au jeu désintéressé de la pensée. Il tend à ruiner définitivement tous les autres mécanismes psychiques et à se substituer à eux dans la résolution des principaux problèmes de la vie...[5]

Breton then points out how many writers have in fact been unwitting surrealists in certain aspects of their writings, a statement which supports exactly the present view of surrealism in Paz's work: 'Swift est surréaliste dans la méchanceté. Sade est surréaliste dans le sadisme . . .' (*Manifestes*, 41).

Because surrealism became for its true adherents so much a way of life and an all-pervading outlook, it is most easily discussed in purely literary terms if broken down into some of the elements most crucial to it. Paz's work can then be examined in more concentrated focus. Thus three categories seem most important as common denominators in surrealism proper and in Paz's poetry: emphasis on the word, the treatment of the image, and the figure of the double, crucial to exploration of the psyche. Naturally surrealism did not depend exclusively upon these three basic approaches; categories galore can be isolated within the movement, from metaphysical systems to creeds of social action. It is merely to avoid dissipation that these three have been chosen as links between Paz in his surrealist mode and the hard-core movement which guided him. Paz was surrealist in technique as and when it suited him, using depersonalization of emotion and dislocation of image to heighten the anguish which he was communicating through the poem. It could even be said of Paz, as Paul Ilie has said of Cernuda, that he is 'a surrealist only to the extent that his compositional needs are being satisfied . . . Indeed we may almost speak of an aesthetic accidentalism, an expedient borrowing of techniques from the French school simply because they are the most appropriate means available for the immediate context.'[6] Given the affinity which Paz feels for Cernuda's poetry, this remark seems particularly applicable to his also.[7]

THE WORD

The Surrealists tried to restore to the word its original purity, a preoccupation in which Mallarmé had preceded them when he claimed that one must 'donner un sens plus pur aux mots de la tribu',[8] though his active verb 'donner' does not apply to the Surrealists. They saw the process more as a removal of a falsifying exterior,[9] and the word as source of the energy which alone could do justice to the surrealist vision. It was this energy which all their techniques strove to release. This awareness of language as such has entered the bloodstream of contemporary poetry, as testified by Sartre among many others: 'L'homme qui parle est au delà des mots, près de l'objet; le poète est en deçà. Pour le premier, ils sont domestiques; pour le second, ils restent à l'état sauvage.'[10] The liberty which the Surrealists demand for the imagination must be realized through the power of the word.

There is an obvious desire in surrealism to step beyond the bounds of the human condition. In this respect there exists a continuity between the Surrealists and the 'Orphic' poets, Nerval,

Hugo, Baudelaire, and Rimbaud, with their efforts to cut through the limitations of the conscious mind.[11] Surrealists were drawn by a desire for transcendence in that their subjectivity and introspection led them through realms of the unconscious from which emergence was the prize of anguish. Yet the 'surreal' is not the 'super-natural', and many Surrealists denied the idea of God while feeling drawn to some awareness of the Infinite.[12] The resolution of resultant tensions between the conscious and the unconscious and between the imagination and the reason occurred for the artist in the possibility of creation. Where the expression of inner visions was possible the psychic balance was restored. Where the conflict became too great between the creative impulse and the imperfection of the medium, alienation took place, silence in the case of Rimbaud, madness in that of Antonin Artaud. The word, then, is not only the means by which the poet descends into the unconscious depths of his mind, formulating for himself and for others the obscure impulses found there, but also the vital medium of adjustment by which man retains contact with both the inner and the outer worlds. Hence the obvious connections between surrealism and psycho-analysis, with similar emphasis on dreams and on the verbal expression of these dreams as well. In both cases the word is clearly the means of survival.

Paz's poetry from first to last shows his obsession with his medium. His early collection, *A la orilla del mundo* (Mexico, 1942), opens with the poem 'Palabra' (*Lib.* 31–2), which elevates language to the mystical heights of the sacramental:

> Palabra, una palabra,
> la última y primera,
> la que callamos siempre,
> la que siempre decimos,
> sacramento y ceniza.
>
> (*Lib.* 32)

His poetry from here on abounds in similar expressions of frustration at the sheer impossibility of there ever existing a sufficiently viable bridge between the experience and the expression of it. Yet talking about the frustration is also conquering it, and the very form given to the despair is the vehicle of salvation. Thus the bridge which sanity demands between the ineffable and the attempt to express it is created even by cries of despair at the impossibility of the task. In the state of mind which accompanies

Paz's surrealist works this is the cry most often heard, and it becomes more poignant through the abandonment of logical discourse which surrealism prescribed.

The whole first section of *¿Aguila o sol?* in fact deals with the nature of the poet's task. 'Trabajos del poeta' (*Lib.* 147–58) is the longest single confrontation of the poet and the word in a struggle which Paz sums up in the small preface which precedes it: '*Ayer, investido de plenos poderes, escribía con fluidez sobre cualquier hoja disponible . . . Hoy lucho a solas con una palabra. La que me pertenece, a la que pertenezco: ¿cara o cruz, águila o sol?*' (*Lib.* 146). The two most impressive facts about this struggle are the personification of the words as assailants (and consequent depersonalization of the poet) and the extraordinary verbal agility in which it is described. Words are in fact the challengers on two levels: the imaginary, which lines them up in fantastic battle array, and the technical, in which the poet literally twists, distorts, and remakes all the components of language to suit his ends. All sixteen sections involve a narrator who gives a first-person account of his trials and torments and whose presence provides the unity of the work. Thematically the work can be discussed in three divisions, though the transitions are so smooth that no distinct breaks occur. But for convenience Sections I to VII may be dealt with as a first theme, divided from their development (Sections IX to XI) by the insomnia of Section VIII. The last five sections, XII to XVI, link the inner sufferings of the narrator to the wider arena of suffering around him.

The frustrations of the narrator in the first unit are twofold. First he is prey to attack by myriads of unwanted elements of language which catch him unawares and force themselves and the nightmare they conceptualize into his consciousness. They present themselves 'desgreñados al alba y pálidos a medianoche . . dientes feroces, voces roncas, todos ojos de bocaza' (*Lib.* 147). They must be fought off, or else they will take control and the consequences will be disastrous. Sections I and II thus show the conscious mind receptive to the impulses of the subconscious and aware of the horrors and the treasures of that realm: 'También debo decir que ciertos días arden, brillan, ondulan, se despliegan o repliegan . . .' (*Lib.* 148). The narrator faces the teleological issue raised by this contamination[13] of the conscious by the unconscious mind: is it providential design or mere fortuitousness which governs this invasion of the psyche? Secondly, there is the urgent need for the right word which will be the poet's bridge back into the mysteries of the imagination and out into the world of human contact. This Word, which Paz capitalizes to add an element of sublimity, comes in moments of silence or inattentiveness, and must be seized if this is possible. Often, as in Section III, the narrator misses his chance: 'Lo inesperado del encuentro me paralizó por un segundo, que fue suficiente para darle tiempo de volver a la noche' (*Lib.* 149).

Section IV explores silence, a silence pulsing with the rhythm which links all layers of creation, from the heart of man to the waves of the sea. Section V breaks the cosmic mood in a brilliant tussle between narrator and language: 'Te desfondo a fondo, te desfundo de tu fundamento. Traquetea tráquea aquea. El carrascaloso se rasca la costra de caspa. Doña campamocha se atasca, tarasca' (*Lib.* 150). Words are coined, rhymed, used alliteratively, played with, and mangled as the narrator bests his adversary. The result is whirlwind chaos ending in breathless mastery: 'Jadeo, penduleo desguanguilado, jadeo.'

The first unit ends with two moments of introspection. In Section VI the narrator considers the disillusionment and the grief of the purification which those who serve poetry must go through. No other process will create the empty expectancy where the Word may some day be heard. The sacrifice of identity must be made, for rewards which are doubtful: 'A veces, una tarde cualquiera, un día sin nombre, cae una Palabra, que se posa levemente sobre esa tierra sin pasado. El pájaro es feroz y acaso te sacará los ojos. Acaso, más tarde, vendrán otros' (*Lib.* 151). Section VII is concerned with words which by their numbers exclude the one magic syllable. The narrator is writing on and on until he realizes that 'un simple monosílabo bastaría para hacer saltar al mundo'. Yet he has cluttered himself with the inessential so that there is no longer room for what would take him to the heart of things.

After the anguish of insomniac introversion in Section VIII, the three sections of the second unit develop in different ways the power of man over language. Section IX picks up the earlier personification of words as inhabitants of some monstrous otherregion who can be manhandled and debased at will once they have been cowed into submission: 'A la palabra odio la alimento con basuras durante años, hasta que estalla en una hermosa explosión purulenta, que infecta por un siglo el lenguaje' (*Lib.* 154). Next the narrator repudiates traditional beliefs along with traditional language, while dreaming up a new fabrication of words which will wipe out the old and clear the ground for a new order: 'Hoy sueño un lenguaje de cuchillos y picos, de ácidos y llamas. Un lenguaje de látigos. Para execrar, exasperar, excomulgar, expulsar . . .' (*Lib.* 155). And finally the fantasy of the word 'Cri' which becomes an elusive will-o'-the-wisp, drawing the hunter-fisherman after it, but never caught, again symbolic of the tantalizing promise of that one word which, if found, will provide a key to all secrets.

The third unit widens the horizons by moving both deeper into the narrator's psyche and further out into the surrounding world. Sections XII and XIV are moments of intense introspection in which preoccupation with language is replaced by deeper feelings of spiritual anguish. The alternating sections move outwards to the sufferings of the narrator's unnamed country, first with the touching parable of Tilantlán, and secondly in a lament for a people whom even hope has passed by: 'Todas las palabras han muerto de sed. Nadie podrá alimentarse con estos restos pulidos . . . Esperanza, águila famélica, déjame sobre esta roca parecida al silencio' (*Lib.* 158). The last section transcends the struggle with language itself to arrive at the implications of speech, and the responsibilities of the artist: '. . . tú, mi Grito, surtidor de plumas de fuego, herida resonante y vasta como el desprendimiento de un planeta del cuerpo de una estrella . . .' (*Lib.* 158). The final justification of the 'trabajos del poeta' is here not only an artistic but a humanitarian one. The inner world of the imagination has been explored and allowed to enrich the workings of the conscious mind. Then the resources of both have been allowed to combine in a universal plea which takes the poet back out from surreality into the world of concrete reality around him. The result has not been an escape, but an enrichment of commitment.

Many poems in *Salamandra* deal in a purely literary or metaphysical framework with the poet's struggle to govern his idiom. Paz's exploration of his Mexican roots does not end after 'Piedra de sol', but recedes into wider concerns. Certainly preoccupations with the creative function of the poet grow more obvious. In 'Disparo' (*Sal.* 21–2) the struggle with language is couched in a series of images which treat the word as an entity with its own energy and animation. It leaps ahead of thought and sound, like a horse ahead of the wind, 'Como un novillo de azufre'. It leaps through the night to lose itself in the sleeping poet's brain. Now the metaphors grow wilder and human anatomy mingles with its surroundings, while sensations of sight and touch are called into play:

> En la cara del árbol el tatuaje escarlata. . .
> En la espalda del muro el tatuaje de hielo
> En el sexo de la iglesia el tatuaje eléctrico. . .
>
> (*Sal.* 21)

The image of the wild beast returns but gives way to that of the sunflower turning towards whiteness, 'Hasta el grito hasta el basta'. Sound and sight fuse in contorted images—'la firma del sin nombre', 'el grito que ciega', 'la imagen que ríe', and the word which 'revienta las palabras'. And the poem ends with seven vertiginous lines of imagery in which one female figure follows another—'la desaparecida en mitad del abrazo . . .', 'la mendiga profética'—until the final release:

> la muchacha que en mitad de la vida
> me despierta y me dice *acuérdate*
>
> (*Sal.* 22)

It is as always for this poet: the poetic faculty itself provides the moment of awakening from the nightmare. There is the pain of initiation, in this case of struggle with incoherence or with the inexpressible, and there is the eventual crystallization of the poem itself which, along with passion and the plenitude of Nature, shows man's transcendence of the limitations of solitude, alienation, and silence.

There are two pairs of poems in *Salamandra* which emerge in very different ways from Paz's need to examine the links between himself, his experiences, and his language. The first pair, 'La palabra escrita' (*Sal.* 29–30) and 'La palabra dicha' (*Sal.* 31–2), experiment with the naming process itself, a self-conscious manipulation of the machinery of language. 'Aspiración' (*Sal.* 50–1) and 'Espiración' (*Sal.* 52–3) use language experimentation as an end in itself, ignoring the means. But both pairs depend upon the ability of the artist to exploit his medium, just as the process was described in 'Trabajos del poeta'. Behind all four poems—and these are chosen merely as examples of a continuing process— lies the conviction cherished by the Surrealists that language could be a tool used to reach and express the subconscious side of the mind. Words, if allowed to emerge from free association of sounds and fantasies, provide one of the most important keys to that integration of the real and the 'surreal' at which surrealism aimed.

Such premisses do not make for easily explicated poems. Both pairs depend on antithetical concepts and are related formally, but at this point comparisons cease to be valid. 'La palabra escrita' is a poem so cryptic in form that it opens itself to many depths of interpretation. There is a creative inspiration, be it on the aesthetic level of the poet or the mystical plane of God, or a combination of both, which provides a leitmotiv recurring six times throughout this comparatively short (thirty-one lines) poem. This phrase, 'Ya escrita la primera / Palabra', is the only one not parenthesized, and it is never made into a complete sentence. Instead it is complemented by what might be called the self-evident reality as opposed to the ontological: parenthetical portions of a scene which involves the sun and a face both reflected in a well. Into this well a stone, objective correlative of the word, is dropped, with the consequent breaking up of the reflected images. When the ripples cease the images return, and the stone/word lies forgotten at the bottom. The poem ends with the antithesis between the absolute first Word and the finite reality which our language can grasp:

> Ya escrita la primera
> Palabra (sigue,
> No hay más palabras que las de la cuenta)
> (*Sal.* 30)

'La palabra dicha' cuts through the polemics of the linguists, following the word from the page into the intricacies of the ear to final silence. On the page the word is frozen like a 'labrada estalactita'; when it frees itself its concept bridges the gulf 'Del silencio al grito'. But in the labyrinth of the ear sound patterns confuse meanings and the mind is side-tracked into senseless games: 'lamenta la mente. / De menta demente . . .' (*Sal.* 32). This chaos distorts the cry which language was to express so that it goes unheard, 'grito / Desoído'. There is only one escape—the way of innocence and silence: 'Para hablar aprende a callar.' Language, as poets and mystics alike learn through anguish, is at best a distortion of the absolute in whatever terms its intuition is felt.

'Aspiración' and 'Espiración' are held together as complementary pieces by a loose web of antithetical developments of a few common themes, and by a formal similarity which seems almost whimsical. Both have three parts, the first two consisting of two five-line stanzas of hendecasyllables interspersed in 'Aspiración' with seven-syllable lines. The third section of both is in unrhymed sonnet form and both start with lines which contain an almost identical word-play. In brief, 'Aspiración' finds the poet divorced from outer reality, aware of memory as the only link with existence on this or any other plane. Memory is his defence against 'la hora y su resaca', and it alone asserts the reality of physical existence, be it his or another's: 'Tu cuerpo es la memoria de mis huesos.' The 'sonnet' opens with an amalgam of earlier themes of shade and sun: 'Sombra del sol / Solombra segadora.' The burden of vitality which memory bears descends now upon the words in which this assertion is expressed. The ear is carried by alliteration and assonance, *s*, *n*, and *a* sounds in the first quatrain, *m*, *n*, and *a* in the second. Words are coined in order that sound may carry a meaning in as valid a way as does sense: 'Mas la memoria desmembrada nada / Desde los nacederos de su nada . . .' (*Sal.* 51). Plays on words ('Nada [i.e. it swims] contra la nada'), paradox ('Sentido sin sentido'), daring images ('Pentecostés palabra sin palabras'), and more alliteration ('Lengua de fuego fosforece el agua') all accumulate until the climactic interplay of sound and sense of the last tercet:

> Sentido sin sentido No pensado
> Pensar que transfigura la memoria
> El resto es un manojo de centellas.
>
> (*Sal.* 51)

The reader is left dazzled by impossible imagery and bewildered by paradox, but aware that the poem offers an affirmation of some lasting element in the human spirit.

'Espiración' is the descent from this peak. Its first part picks up motifs from 'Aspiración'—the white shadows of the day, and the existence of memory—but the image has changed. Memory is now a 'torre hendida, / Pausa vacía entre dos claridades'. The city has become disembodied, and the outer world invisible. Does memory provide a defence? '¿En tu memoria / Serán mis huesos tiempo incandescente?' The image of death dominates the second section, death in its macabre, skeletal manifestation. There is no defence against physical decay, and all that love leaves is a 'trazo negro de

la quemadura . . . en lo blanco de los huesos'. The 'sonnet' plays
with the shade–sun paradox of its partner. The order is reversed—
'Sombra de sol' to 'Sol de sombra'—and the sound of 'segadora'
is kept, though a new image is superimposed: 'Solombra cegadora'.
This reinforces the theme of blind eyes which occurred in the
first part of 'Aspiración' and again in its sonnet, but now the poet
insists upon the reverse concept. Though sun and shade blind the
natural vision (i.e. death cuts down physical life), there is an
inner vision which remains: 'Mis ojos han de ver lo nunca visto . . .
El revés de lo visto y de la vista.'

The same word-games (alliteration, assonance, etc.) bring to
the second quatrain the flavour of a burlesque funeral ceremony:
'(Los laúdes del laúdano de loas . . .)', and the last tercet ends in
an irony of verbal play which makes the cryptic last line capable
of a paradoxical doubling of interpretation:

> Lo nunca visto nunca dicho nunca
> Es lo ya dicho el nunca del retruécano
> Vivo me ves y muerto no has de verme
> (*Sal.* 53)

Thus another level of the power of words has been explored,
namely irony, in which plays on words can not only call to mind
varieties of associative meanings, but can also introduce an atmosphere of polyvalency which sets the poem in a context of ambiguity.
This combination of surprising images with verbal experimentation
and irony sums up, I suggest, the surrealist mode as Paz used it.
That is to say that he was not by conviction a Surrealist, and
could use their techniques with the pinch of objectivity which
the ambiguity of this poem suggests. Yet he was well aware of the
pertinence of their tenets and literary methods, and used this mode
as it suited his bent. Precisely for this reason it is possible to
discuss a surrealist mode within the works of a poet who could
never by reason of his eclecticism be pigeon-holed as a Surrealist.

THE IMAGE

The Surrealists wished to revitalize an alienated world by the
spontaneous activity of the imagination. They saw violence and
shock as effective ways to recreate in the adult the immediacy and
totality of vision given to him as a child but later lost by all but

certain 'âmes privilégiées'. The way to this lies through the visual and emotional shock of imagery which calls upon the intuitive world of the imagination. By juxtaposing two distant elements a new element is created, and the world is transformed, becomes more than real, as the image flashes a new light upon the disparities it has fused together. The result is often a 'beauté convulsive', which gives a violent shock to a mind imprisoned in old concepts and conditioned to respond intellectually to its surroundings. Thus surrealism literally causes a revolution in our perceptivity, and an acceptance of imagery which brings to light connections of which the perceiver has been sluggishly unaware. Lautréamont's famous image of 'la rencontre fortuite sur une table de dissection d'une machine à coudre et d'un parapluie',[14] links literary surrealism to the art of Miró, Magritte, Dali, and the world of the ready-mades.

This use of the startling image to transform reality is abundant in those volumes of Paz already mentioned. Sometimes creation of an atmosphere is an end in itself, and images in weird and troubling combinations disturb the acceptance of outer reality. ¿Aguila o sol? provides so many examples of such imagery that one chosen at random may be considered representative. 'Lecho de helechos' (Lib. 202) communicates a mood of mystic expectancy by means of a Daliesque landscape. The poet stands at the end of the world, before him a landscape of immense, sleeping, but still sparkling eyes, and there stares at him 'tu mirada última— la mirada que pierde cielo'. Shining scales of glances cover the beach, and a liquid gold wave is receding. The life-force gazing at him becomes a lunar drumskin, a piece of star on the edge of a crater, and the poet seems to hold up reality with the magnetism of his eyes: 'Te sostienen en vilo mis ojos, como la luna a la marea encendida. A tus pies la espuma degollada canta el canto de la noche que empieza' (Lib. 202).

The violent fusion of disparate objects can have more troubling effects, as in 'Entrada en materia', the first poem in Salamandra (9–13). The mood of suffering and alienation which is conveyed by imagery of city life seems to suggest that the 'materia' of the title is an objective correlative for the underworld of the myth of birth and rebirth. The hero must be withdrawn from his normal sphere, his worth tested against forces both alien and dangerous, in order to emerge into the new consciousness to which he is heir.

The initiate, in other words, must earn his right to knowledge of ancient truths by pain and frustration on a physical or a spiritual level.

Like the initiate, the poet stands to gain greater awareness of human and ultra-human truths, but at a price—the price he must pay himself, when he stands as a stranger in his land, faced with an alien society and unacceptable values. The city is Paz's waste land in 'Entrada en materia', and the poem dwells on the paradox of man's spiritual and physical beauty caught in a labyrinth of concrete which echoes the inhumanity of the modern civilized world.

The opening image of this poem is hard and cold, the repeated *r* and *i* sounds of the first line sharp and cruel—'Piedras de ira fría'. The city is bitter and claustrophobic, full of tall houses with saltpetre lips: 'casas podridas en el saco del invierno'.[15] This technique of personification grows more horrible as the human attributes become more shocking:

> Noche de innumerables tetas
> y una sola boca carnicera . . .
> *(Sal.* 9)

The neon lights are decorated with 'guirnaldas de dientes', they blink with 'El guiño obsceno de los números', and in the destroyed night the city becomes synonymous with 'Gatos en celo y pánico de monos'. But inhuman though time and place may be, there is still

> El sagrario del cuerpo
> El arca del espíritu
> Los labios de la herida
> *(Sal.* 9)

The last image (which ends the poem in the first edition) evokes in the reader's mind the triple concept of poet-sufferer-speaker which appeared already in the much more direct image of 'Fuente' (*Lib.* 216–18), and which will reappear in the poignant image of 'Cosante':

> Con la lengua cortada canta
> Sangre sobre la piedra
> El ruiseñor en la muralla
> *(Sal.* 71)

The atmosphere grows more threatening as the invisible tide of fear overtakes 'torres ceñudas . . . sonámbulos palacios . . . graves moles', and brings in evil:

> El mal promiscuo el mal sin nombre
> Todos los nombres del mal
> El mal que tiene todos los nombres. . .
> *(Sal.* 10)

The city becomes a grotesque female figure:

> Entre tus muslos un reloj da la hora
> Demasiado tarde
> Demasiado pronto
> En tu cama de siglos fornican los relojes. . .
> *(Sal.* 10)

Time and place are out of season, and the poet's ears ring with the senseless sounds of the city and the tick of clocks which defeat language.

The moon with its connotations of mystery and magic rises, but is defeated too; it falls 'como un borracho' and is defiled by the 'perros callejeros', by a convoy of trucks, by a cat, and 'Los carniceros se lavan las manos / En el agua de la luna'. The chime of a clock leads to a labyrinthine play on the words 'hora' and 'ahora', as the poet senses himself at a point in time where there is no place for him. He is unable to grasp the immediacy of the moment, yet finds himself trapped in the passage of minutes and hours.

The poem's focus turns to the figure of the poet again, and to Paz's constant preoccupation with language, condemned by 'la conciencia y sus pulpos escribanos' to perpetual inadequacy:

> El tribunal condena lo que escribo
> El tribunal condena lo que callo . . .
> *(Sal.* 11)

To the poet who is caught between the limitations of time and reason, words seem only to construct their own incoherence:

> Una ciudad inmensa y sin sentido
> Un monumento grandioso incoherente
> Babel babel minúscula . . .
> *(Sal.* 12)

But the alternative is silence which 'no es fácil y además no puedo', and furthermore there is a mysticism in the whole process by which things are given their names. Names and nouns interpret the outer world: 'Ejes / anchas espaldas de este mundo'; provide a bulwark against time: 'Lomos que cargan sin esfuerzo al tiempo'; and lead beyond materialism to spiritual regions, though the entry is perilous: 'Puerta puerta condenada'. This concept opens the final moment when the poet fights through the contradictions of temporality and reality to the paradox of the name, which interprets the object by defining its existence, yet in definition proves its own inadequacies. Thus the hold upon outer reality is never secure. Bound in subjectivity, man cannot escape the intangibility of what surrounds him:

> Los nombres no son nombres
> No dicen lo que dicen. . .
> (*Sal.* 13)

Civilization closes around him with 'Piedra sangre esperma / Ira ciudad relojes / Pánico risa pánico'.

There is an emergence from the labyrinth, however, as Paz sees the poet's task:

> Yo he de decir lo que dicen
> El sagario del cuerpo
> El arca del espíritu
> (*Sal.* 13)

The essence of man is a spiritual one, as the images of ciborium and ark make clear, and it will survive, but the pain by which this survival is assured is what is remembered of this poem. Man is seen within the urban society which the civilized world has developed and so highly values, and in which he is crushed and almost annihilated. This inhuman process is expressed by dehumanized imagery made more impressive by the surrealist technique of a startling conjunction of ideas and objects. Thus, inanimate things grow wings and roots, they become alive, but with terrifying attributes—'Garras dientes / Tienen ojos y uñas uñas uñas' (*Sal.* 13). The city is alive with clocks as man is enmeshed in time, but the image shocks: 'Entre tus muslos un reloj da la hora.' It brings to mind at once the concepts of flesh, prostitution, and temporality. Or to pick another example at random, conscience is pictured presiding over a tribunal table with octopus clerks around him.

The moon images show this process in which the world of spirituality and beauty is abused by the crass materialism of today. The moon in Paz's work is often connected with the female principle, as is so often the case in mythology. It also traditionally connotes chastity, mystery, distance from human commerce; and a long line of poetical antecedents condition us in our awareness of its potential symbolism. All the more impressive then, the contrast between the conditioned reaction to the moon and the unsavoury opening simile, and the even blunter punch of the *o*, *e*, and *b* sounds of the fifth line:

> Como un enfermo desangrado se levanta
> La luna
> Sobre las altas azoteas
> La luna
> Como un borracho cae de bruces. . .
>
> (*Sal.* 10)

The harsh *c* continues through the moon metaphors—'perros callejeros', 'un convoy de camiones', 'un gato cruza'—and reaches its climax in the brutality of the butchers who wash their hands in moonlight:

> Los carniceros se lavan las manos
> En el agua de la luna. . .
>
> (*Sal.* 11)

The poet's horror at the ugly facts of existence in a modern world thus is communicated through a surrealist vision of personified objects (the night, the city, the moon) which are alive with the grotesque and fearful characteristics of human or animal life. Style and content are at one in this nightmare sensation of the human being in a world which reduces him to the level of the inhuman—an equation produced precisely by the personification mentioned above. To transmit anguish Paz engages sight, or rather imagination, in a series of contorted transformations of the 'real' to the 'super-real'. That which is seen and recognized is magically changed by its being related to some distant but otherwise perfectly recognizable facet of reality. Thus 'night' given 'countless nipples' begins a chain of associated ideas which leads beyond the real into the depths of the unconscious mind. This unconscious is where lie hidden or half-hidden the nameless fears and atavistic taboos which so well communicate Paz's feeling of alienation both from exterior reality and from the source of poetic inspiration.

Salamandra provides other and different examples of a surrealist use of the image as reconciler of conscious and subconscious levels of reality. A whimsical scene like that of 'Peatón' (*Sal.* 23) is also based upon the emergence of the fantasy world into daylight, here literal, not metaphorical, daylight. The process is objectified and drily told in the third person: a man walks along minding his own business, is stopped by a red light, and looks up. Above the grey roofs 'plateado / Entre los pardos pájaros, / Un pescado volaba'. The light changes and he crosses the street, trying to pick up the chain of thought he has lost:

> Se preguntó al cruzar la calle
> En qué estaba pensando.
> (*Sal.* 23)

The technique of depersonalization in 'Augurios' (*Sal.* 18-19) covers deeply felt emotions, and the disfiguration of the images in this poem correlates with the pain of the poet, out of harmony with the civilization around him. All that he sees tends to the distortion of generosity and love, and to the palliation of the masses: 'Una filantropía que despena', an easy materialism whose comfort anaesthetizes emotion. The weird opening image objectifies the annulment of heroism and love in the bottling of the Cid's daughters:

> Al natural, en cápsulas, abiertas
> O cerradas, ya desalmadas,
> Elvira y doña Sol . . .
> (*Sal.* 18)

To communicate the feeling that humanity is being dulled out of suffering and thus out of awareness, Paz uses a string of images which surprise by their content or their juxtaposition. There is a sedative against everything:

> Contra las erosiones . . .
> Crisis, poetas solitarios auto-
> Críticas, purgas, cismas, putschs, eclipses . . .
> (*Sal.* 18)

The city dehumanizes to the point of ridicule—'Pulgas / Vestidas a la moda'—and Nature herself has been degraded—'En las playas mariscos erotómanos'. Mankind is hell-bent on escaping any kind of sensation but the hedonistic: 'Cura de sueño, orgasmos por teléfono. / Arcoiris portátiles . . .' The ultimate philanthropy will be that which does away with pain. The poet has no need to enter the poem directly, for the deliberate dislocation of the image has carried the experience of nausea and foreboding which it is the purpose of the poem to communicate. The surrealist mode itself induces the anguish which is the real subject of the poem.

THE DOUBLE

One motif in Paz's poetry is most suitably discussed in the context of the surrealist mode, even though it is universal to literature. The theme of the double became characteristic of surrealist aesthetics, though it can certainly not be claimed as their prerogative. Folklore and occultism provide many stories of apparitions which are identical to still-living human beings, and the idea of a second self pervades the most sophisticated as well as the most naïve levels of literature. Because of their faith in the subconscious functions of the human mind as transformers of reality, the Surrealists were attracted by the practices and particularly the philosophy of alchemy. In this, to be sure, they picked up the earlier addiction of such nineteenth-century thinkers and writers as Victor Hugo and Gérard de Nerval, with their interest in magic and the occult. It was the spiritual content of alchemy which fascinated them, what Jung describes as '—the transcendent function, the transformation of personality through the blending and fusion of the noble with the base components, of the differentiated with the inferior functions, of the conscious with the unconscious'.[16] Surrealist poetry often expresses a haunting consciousness of the duality of the human psyche, which allows any facet of man's activity to be called into question or set in a higher frame of reference by his other self.[17] Breton and his colleagues sought deliberately to evoke this other self, as Paz's own words on Breton point out: 'Decir es la actividad más alta: revelar lo escondido, despertar la palabra enterrada, suscitar la aparición de nuestro doble, crear a ese otro que somos y al que nunca dejamos de ser del todo.'[18]

Paz's conception of the double is basic to his poetic vision, and his prose writings repeat the fact again and again: 'La poesía no dice: yo soy tú; dice: mi yo eres tú. La imagen poética es la otredad.'[19] Using only the evidence of his poetry, one becomes aware of the polyvalency of the image of the double for Paz. It acts as an objective correlative for his epistemological uncertainties, for his awareness of the plurality lying behind seemingly simple appearances, and for his vision of the poet who suffers in order to redeem.

In the early *Puerta condenada* (1938–46), included in the second section, 'Calamidades y milagros', of *Libertad bajo palabra*, the young poet returns time and again to a discourse with his other self, as he explores the seeming certainties of reality and finds the emptiness beneath. It is as though the use of a poetic dialectic is the first step towards the paradox of the later works in which preoccupations are similar, but expression so different. 'Pregunta' (*Lib*. 56–8) opens with a direct appeal to spiritual forces which recall Alberti's angels:

> Déjame, sí, déjame, dios o ángel, demonio.
> Déjame a solas, turba angélica,
> solo conmigo, con mi multitud.
>
> (*Lib*. 56)

The poet stands beside one who resembles himself, who contains all opposites, who embraces and wounds, who 'me odia porque yo soy el mismo'. Then Paz apostrophizes this 'aborrecible hermano mío', trying to harmonize his consciousness of all the infinite possibilities of the human spirit with the time-corroded being of every day:

> ¿es el tuyo, tu ser, hecho de horas
> y voraces minutos?
>
> (*Lib*. 57)

The next strophe has a Machado-like ring; the poet returns to a solitary questioning of the inexplicable facts of human existence, body and soul united to form what Paz sees as 'una sola y viva sombra'. An earlier generation of poets echoes in the next three lines—do we dream our own existence to defy time, and are we merely the self we dream ourselves to be?

> ¿Y somos esa imagen que soñamos,
> sueños al tiempo hurtados,
> sueños del tiempo por burlar al tiempo?
>
> (*Lib*. 57)

Alone, the poet works through layers of appearances to reach the essence of his personality. He passes beneath words, deceiving externals, and the illusions of temporal reality, only to find his very existence disappearing before his eyes, like a mirror which reflects another mirror-image to eternity:

> me voy borrando todo,
> me voy haciendo un vago signo sobre el agua,
> espejo en un espejo.
>
> *(Lib. 58)*

'La caída', in the same volume *(Lib.* 61–2), is another cry of existential anguish. The essence of the poet's despair is time, which threatens all existence, returning life to non-life in an inexorable, silent process. The poet sees himself

> En el abismo de mi ser nativo,
> en mi nada primer, me desvivo:
> yo mismo frente a mí, ya devorado.
>
> *(Lib. 62)*

Ultimately only reason offers him cold comfort, and 'la inefable / y helada intimidad de su vacío'.

The double, who acts as a mirror-image showing the poet truths at which he can otherwise only guess, appears again in 'Los crepúsculos de la ciudad', a series of sonnets also in *Puerta condenada (Lib.* 63–6). Again the poet is imprisoned in time's destructiveness, and sees no salvation or solace:

> Vuelvo el rostro: no soy sino la estela
> de mí mismo, la ausencia que deserto,
> el eco del silencio de mi grito.
>
> *(Lib. 65)*

In these poems the double bears witness to the poet of the anguish and hopelessness of existence. Epistemological doubt and a sense of time draw the poet into a labyrinth from which he does not find escape, and in which his only companion is an *alter ego* doomed to the same fate as himself. This poet has found no transcendence; he has desperately sought the way to rebirth, but so far with no success. He has rejected traditional religion, the myths of older civilizations have no strength to give him, and so far he has not found for himself any personal release from the temporal world which haunts him. The existential torment of this spirit is a true initiatory rite.

In *¿Águila o sol?* there are two curious pieces which deal with the poet's awareness of a splintering of his personality. In neither case is the second self defined simply as a double; both poems depart from complex conceptions and move through layers of introspection to give at the last some notion of the ambiguity of the human psyche. Thus these prose poems objectify the exploration of the subconscious which was the guiding principle of surrealism. The narrator faces the dark impulses of his mind by personifying them, in slightly different ways which are parallel manifestations of the same process. This process is basically one of integration, since recognizing the *alter ego* in its various guises is the first step towards unifying the divided self. And this alone can produce the balance of conscious and subconscious urges which is needed to combat the alienating business of existence in a modern world.

'Antes de dormir' (*Lib*. 162–5) is a monologue directed by the poet at the invisible being whom he feels sharing and influencing his existence. This being is a disquieting one, since it seems to escape the limits of the rational and set up an atavistic base of prejudices, 'muralla circular que defiende dos o tres certidumbres'. The unseen presence looks through the narrator's eyes, and its gaze awakens an answering animism in the objects round about. But such demands are too strong, and the narrator threatens to get rid of this other self for ever. Of course he cannot, and the monologue evolves into self-justification in an attempt to integrate these complementary parts of the personality. The outer self, the narrator, must face the world and its exigencies. The inner self withdraws from such pressures and has to be coaxed and persuaded to re-emerge. In times of introspection, its presence is felt again, evidence of a spiritual life which submerges but does not disappear: 'penetras por la hendidura de la tristeza o por la brecha de la alegría, te sirves del sueño y de la vigilia, del espejo y del muro, del beso y de la lágrima' (*Lib*. 163). When physical life ends and the useless battle against time is over, the inner self will be in sole possession of the field. The narrator's ultimate confession is that life has given him only the awareness of his inner self— 'solo te tengo a ti'. But there may be an endless chain of such dependence upon an inner presence. It may not be so simple to reach the absolute: '. . . a mí también me ha desvelado la posibilidad de que tú seas de otro, que a su vez sería de otro, hasta no acabar nunca . . . No, si tu eres otro: ¿quién seria yo?' (*Lib*. 164). Thus essentially both selves depend upon each other for validity. The conscious self cannot be considered authentic and the inner self as the shadow; nor can the life of the spirit provide total justification for the outer person who must face the world. Both share the same roots ('tú también tuviste una infancia solitaria y ardiente'), and although the conscious mind may often mistake the nature of subconscious urges, the integration of both levels is needed for inner harmony: 'no te siento como el que fui sino como el que voy a ser, como el que está siendo.' The narrator probes and questions, trying to move from this insight to categoric certainty—'¿Quién eres?' But cajolement and vilification both fail. The interminable dialogue in which one is always silent is that of life. Only full acceptance of self, and sleep, can interrupt this one-sided dialectic: 'No me mires: cierra los ojos, para que yo también pueda cerrarlos. Todavía no puedo acostumbrarme a tu mirada sin ojos' (*Lib.* 165).

The second prose poem, 'Carta a dos desconocidas' (*Lib.* 171–3), is different in degree though not in kind. The shadow self is here intuited as feminine, which seems to relate it with other obvious expressions of Paz's search for the *anima* principle, 'Piedra de sol', for example. The narrator speaks to this female presence which comes to him with greatest poignancy at moments of desperation when he feels both the horror of material emptiness and the anguish of existence: '. . . el invisible precipicio que en ocasiones se abre frente a mí, la gran boca maternal de la ausencia . . . todo, en fin, lo que me enseña que no soy sino una ausencia que se despeña, me revelaba . . . tu presencia' (*Lib.* 171–2). The encounter becomes a triangle when the second 'desconocida', perhaps the personification of loved womanhood, appears. The narrator is led to her by his companion, and 'soy para ella lo que tú fuiste para mí'. Yet the pursuit of the beloved is essentially that of the 'presencia'. Thus in woman the narrator is seeking that shadow self, the *anima*, which he needs to complete his being. Physical love can unite him with another body, but not with the wholeness which he is looking for. True life will come 'Si alguna vez acabo de caer, allá, del otro lado del caer . . .' And this life, perhaps, is only another way of disguising death. The *anima* may after all return to give wholeness to his being in the moment when death ends all fragmentation: 'Pero acaso todo esto no sea sino una vieja manera de llamar a la muerte. La muerte que nació conmigo y que me ha dejado para habitar otro cuerpo' (*Lib.* 173). The appeal of both pieces is for an integration of the self to face the exigencies of life and the urges of the subconscious. Both follow the path of self-discovery into the recesses of the mind. Both recognize fragmentations of the personality which demand exploration and expression before inner order and balance can be regained. Such were, among others, the impulses behind surrealism, for, to quote Breton, surrealism 'tend a la récupération totale de notre force psychique par un moyen qui est la descente vertigineuse en nous, l'illumination systématique des lieux cachés et l'obscurcissement progressif des autres lieux'.[20]

In 1950, at Avignon, Paz wrote 'Fuente', a poem which appeared in *La estación violenta* (*Lib.* 216–18). The image of the double is used, along with a suffering image, but with a difference which shows Paz moving towards an escape from the sense of time of the earlier poems into a mythological interpretation of poetic inspiration. The poet is the sacrificial victim who is destroyed in the battle with hostile powers, but by his death frees the spirit of poetry and redeems the alien world. The moment of the poem is noon,[21] and the atmosphere is one of expectancy. Like several other poems of the same volume, the lines are long and the rhythm rolling and powerful. The poet senses a presence, a promise of some transcendental happening in which time will shatter and reveal some deeper meaning. But the promise seems false and the expectancy cheated. No easy certainty dispels his questioning, though he persists until the old wounds heal, the scars almost disappear, and the meaning of the moment seems lost. Yet there is a transcendence, in very special terms. There is a privileged being (one recalls the 'âmes privilégiées' of Breton) who rises from his own delirium, wounded, yet

> . . . de su frente hendida brota un último pájaro.
> Es el doble de sí mismo,
> el joven que cada cien años vuelve a decir unas
> palabras, siempre las mismas. . . .
> (*Lib.* 218)

The sacrifice must be made, Christ-like, but redemption—for Paz, poetry—remains:

> En el centro de la plaza la rota cabeza del poeta es
> una fuente.
> La fuente canta para todos.
> (*Lib.* 218)

This mysterious potentiality of the double to reveal truths of a spiritual nature haunts even the simplest of Paz's poems which contain this motif. 'La calle' of *Puerta condenada* (*Lib.* 73) recalls 'Aquí' of *Salamandra* (*Sal.* 17), although the earlier work has much of the despair of the poems from the same volume discussed above. In both poems the setting is a street where the poet becomes aware of another presence, a shadow self in 'La calle', in 'Aquí' an echo of his own footsteps in a street, 'Donde / Sólo es real la niebla'. In *Ladera Este* one short poem recalls Breton's poem 'Rideau, rideau',[22] and the earlier *Picture of Dorian Gray*,[23] with an even more macabre twist. The mask-face has hidden the real self from the world until

> Su cara
> Hoy tiene las arrugas de esa cara.
> Sus arrugas no tienen cara.
>
> (*L.E.* 31)

To end this discussion of the double in Paz's surrealist mode, a quotation from one of the major poems of *Ladera Este*, 'Cuento de dos jardines' (*L.E.* 130–41), is particularly apt. I have tried to show how Paz's obvious kinship with surrealism belongs to a definite period and expresses a definite state of mind. In the latest poems (those of *Ladera Este*) both the state of mind and the expression are transcended in poems where paradox leads to the threshold of mysticism. The undifferentiated vision of such poems transforms also Paz's use of the motif of the double. The rebirth so painfully sought brings with it the amalgamation of the *ego* and the *alter ego* in a more highly developed consciousness, and this, I believe, is what lies behind these lines:

> Nadie acaba en sí mismo.
> Un todo cada uno
> En otro todo,
> En otro uno:
> Constelaciones.
>
> (*L.E.* 134)

Surrealism provided Paz with a style peculiarly suited to the chaos which in the cosmological myths precedes creation and form, and in the poet's psychological reference expresses the alienation from mankind and from himself which must be suffered in order to be transcended. It is a double trauma, or more exactly is expressed as such, since the poet and the man are homologous. The question is one of focus: Paz sometimes emphasizes the common nature of man as experienced by himself, at others he dwells upon his predicament as writer. Then the general chaos becomes the plight of the creative artist seeking form and expression in a world without paradigms. In the over-all view of his work surrealism seems to fulfil for Paz at one stage what paradox will do at another. That is, surrealism with its emphasis on integrating the conscious and the subconscious, the 'real' and the 'super-real', provides a dialectic which leads to unity or, in Hegelian terms, through thesis and antithesis to synthesis. It is not that the process is neatly laid out each time as this generalization might imply. The synthesis, like the mythic rebirth, is not always achieved, and the experiences communicated by the poems mark stages within this pattern which must be suffered in their own terms. Yet the final vision is the same, however expressed, whether as Jungian individuation, or Buddhist union with the One Mind, or Breton's 'point sublime', living centre of the world's unity.

III

THE SEMIOTIC MODE

W ITHIN the diversity of Octavio Paz's poetic world lies an inner cohesion which this study attempts to describe. Given the intuitive nature of creative art which picks up where discursive language leaves off, and given also the paradox of poetry, obliged to use for non-rational communication the same ingredients as does rational discourse, the impossibility of the critic's task is basically insurmountable. Yet his role is that of intermediary and his object is to enhance the work by isolating it within a set of detached as well as emotional responses. With these facts in mind, a discussion of the patterns underlying the poet's vision may clarify and perhaps deepen the reader's instinctive reaction to the individual poems as to the total *œuvre*. The corpus of Paz's poetry still expands physically by new production, its limits as yet unfixed in time, yet the work of all poets, living or dead, exists independently as an organic entity capable of immeasureable expansion in its spiritual sphere which is the mind of man. Every poet builds for himself a linguistic edifice of changing density, changing because language itself develops, because the man within the poet grows, and because every reader comes equipped with his own more or less adequate imagination, ear, and perception. Yet with all its shifts in height and depth and changes of mood and colour, the uniqueness of each edifice remains recognizable because of the structure around which it is built. Of this structure the most fundamental aspect is the language which the poet fabricates as a web to contain himself and his reality.

The development in Paz's poetic language has already been touched on in the discussion of the mythic mode spanning his poetic output, and the surrealist mode which isolates the atmosphere indicative of a certain stage in his life and thought. The semiotic mode concerns a very particular atmosphere which pervades his work from first to last and is dependent upon a private vocabulary. This vocabulary is a constant factor around which style and theme change, but whose essence remains the same—the same in kind, that is, for there is a difference in degree which accompanies the spiritual growth of the man himself. The recurrence of specific words calls up in the mind of the reader a series of motifs central to Paz's poetic vision, motifs expressing the most intimate intuitions of which his poetry is woven.

The ability of the same words to indicate spiritual change is one of the strange facts about language itself, a fact which linguists and critics of poetry have attempted to schematize. Dámaso Alonso took exception to Saussure's definition of *signo* as meaning both *significante* and *significado*, and separated the two latter.[1] Saussure used *significante* as meaning the acoustic image, and *significado* as the concept aroused by this image. The sign, i.e. the word, was thus a composite of acoustic image and concept. Dámaso Alonso (though ignoring Saussure's distinction between 'language' and 'speech', the *lengua / habla* dichotomy) deepens this analysis. *Significante* becomes sound and acoustic image combined, and because it emerges from the pysche of the speaker, it draws upon multiple associations both conceptual and synaesthetic. It arouses in the hearer an equally dense web of responses, and this *carga compleja* is the *significado*. Thus both *significante* and *significado* become complex entities composed of a series of associative nuances. Stephen Ullmann uses simpler terminology by calling the *significante* 'name' and *significado* 'sense', and the web of connotations which both occasion he calls the 'associative field'.[2] The differences in associative field for both poet and reader are what allow Paz's personal vocabulary to acquire its accumulative meanings. 'Names' carry motifs which serve as unifying factors in the total fabric of his work, deepening in significance as the word itself draws on more of the psychic resources of both creator and participator. This process, at once linguistic and spiritual, is what I have called the semiotic mode.

In attempting to translate into discursive language experiences conveyed by recurrent motifs, it becomes obvious that the nature of the poet's search is epistemological. Denied or unable to find faith in religious creeds, he still functions as a metaphysical being, seeking transcendence through full acceptance of the physical universe. When the desired vision is denied him, he feels surrounded by mirrors which reflect his own limited self, or which shatter, or worse yet, reveal a nothingness empty of hope. Yet these moods are displaced by moments, of which noon is often one, when the outer world of appearances promises the possibility of a spiritual break-through. When this happens the poet glimpses a presence, time loses its meaning, and a transparent moment, 'un instante', takes him into the secret heart of things. He then reaches the 'other shore', a metaphor which binds Paz's private experience to one of the universal spiritual truths as discussed in Chapter I. Thus the importance to Paz of the mythic cycle of life–death–rebirth seems evident in the reappearance throughout his poems of 'instante', 'presencia', 'transparencia', 'plenitud', 'orilla', to quote the most obvious cases. In the moment of enlightenment the universe (or language of the loved one) yields to a transfigured consciousness an awareness of unity which can be compared only to a mystical experience. These glimpses of light, truth, or whatever term of undifferentiation is used, flash out from Paz's earliest poems onwards, with an attendant sense of order and peace when they are achieved, and a consequent frustration when they are not. Examination of even a few of these keywords will help to show the growing depth and beauty of Paz's poetic world.

INSTANTE

The imprisoning effect of time upon man has been and will always be one of the most inexorable conditions of human life. It is a trammel which constantly chafes and frustrates those who become aware of the paradox of the life of the mind, itself timeless, in a body which is finite and will die. Myth is the form by which the mind seeks to order its own timelessness, since only through form can perception be complete. The myths of primitive peoples and the higher religions of East and West alike all tend to the presentation in some understandable form of the realm beyond, called by various names: eternity, *sunyata*, *illud tempus*, paradise, and so on. Art, *sui generis*, removes us from one time-sphere into another. It is more than disbelief which we suspend in the theatre, for instance; we enter into a time-sphere imposed by an artist who conveys to us an experience which we can only describe as creative. While this creative experience lasts, the narrowness of daily life and human time is replaced by an awareness of some intricately wrought composure. There is, then, a sense in which every work of art creates its own 'instante', for it is itself the awareness in the artist of a new consciousness. This consciousness steps outside time, and in it the reader, or listener, or viewer, as the case may be, must participate to the best of his ability, drawing from the depths of experiences already undergone or perceptions still latent within him. So the emergence of the poem on the page is already the creation of a magic moment, akin to the timelessness sought by myth and by religion.

Within this new time-dimension the poet's search for another reality is set in relief. The 'instante' sought and sometimes found is the enlightenment of all transcendental experiences, and preoccupation with it runs through the three volumes of Paz's poetry.[3] In 'Apuntes del insomnio' (*Lib.* 45) the moment is glimpsed and escapes, leaving the poet to face a future as unrelenting as a blank wall. This is a simple, understated poem from 1944, and opens directly with the poet's fear that time will eat away his life if he cannot escape:

> Roe el reloj
> mi corazón,
> buitre no, sino ratón.
>
> (*Lib.* 45)

The feeling of release comes too easily, though, and proves an illusion:

> En la cima del instante
> me dije: 'Ya soy eterno
> en la plenitud del tiempo.'
> Y el instante se caía
> en otro, abismo sin tiempo.
>
> (*Lib.* 45)

And the future looms up, unavoidable; this time there has been no escape.

The intense moment or 'instante' proves less illusory when it is discovered in love and the shared experience of sexual passion. Poem after poem in *Libertad bajo palabra* sings of the opening up of time through erotic union with the body of a woman. In 'Piedra nativa' (*Lib.* 127–9) the theme of fertility binds woman and Nature. The promise of the land is fulfilled when 'Una muchacha ríe a la entrada del día', and the pulsing of new life returns to transfigured Nature:

En el calor se afila el instante dichoso
Agua tierra y sol son un solo cuerpo
La hora y su campana se disuelven
Las piedras los paisajes se evaporan

. . . . .

Música despeñada
Y ardemos y no dejamos huella
(*Lib.* 129)

In 'Elogio' (*Lib.* 132–3) all Nature grows in an immense climax
at the sight of the loved one's face:

Como el día y el fruto y la ola, como el tiempo que
madura un año para dar un instante de belleza y
colmarse a sí mismo con esa dicha instantánea,
La vi una tarde y una mañana y un mediodía y otra tarde
y otra y otra . . . (*Lib.* 132)

And in 'Estrella interior' the woman's body is a 'transparente
monumento / Donde el instante brilla y se repite / Y se abisma
en sí mismo y nunca se consume' (*Lib.* 135).
'Semillas para un himno' (*Lib.* 137–9) describes the very nature
of time itself, immeasurable by reason of its inconstancy:

(pero es verdad que el tiempo no se mide
Hay instantes que estallan y son astros
Otros son un río detenido y unos árboles fijos
Otros son ese mismo río arrasando los mismos árboles)
(*Lib.* 137)

Moments of illumination, like those things which inspire them
('Dos o tres nubes de cristal de roca . . . Islas en llamas en mitad
del Pacífico . . .') are undeserved blessings, unforeseen and unfor-
seeable in a world 'condenada a repetirse sin tregua', where we
are unworthy by our human limitations of such vision. Yet such
moments arrive, 'Instantáneas / Imprevistas cifras del mundo',
and another reality is perceived through them 'Por un instante
están los nombres habitados . . .' (*Lib.* 139).
The same feeling of a moment mystically filled with a higher
meaning reappears time and again in Paz's poetry from this point
onwards, most obviously in 'Piedra de sol'. This poem has already
been discussed at length, so it will be more interesting to isolate
this moment in two poems very close to 'Piedra de sol' in time,

'¿No hay salida?' (*Lib*. 226–9) and 'El río' (*Lib*. 229–32), both from *La estación violenta* of 1957.

'¿No hay salida?' begins with the poet's sense of imprisonment which takes various forms; he feels his thought enclosed in 'las aguas estancadas del lenguaje', unable to find expression in images and words—'y una a una desertan las imágenes, una a una las palabras se cubren el rostro.' His sense of time also holds him captive and he realizes the futility of living for the past and the future:

> Pasó ya el tiempo de esperar la llegada del tiempo, el
>   tiempo de ayer, hoy y mañana,
> ayer es hoy, mañana es hoy, hoy todo es hoy, salió de
>   pronto de sí mismo y me mira . . .
>   (*Lib*. 227)

He is forced to accept as reality the present moment with all that such an acceptance imposes upon the human spirit. He is enclosed in space, also, standing in the centre of the room as in the centre of time and of his thoughts, and the essence of the now is all that he can hold to: 'todo se ha cerrado sobre sí mismo, he vuelto adonde empecé, todo es hoy y para siempre.' There is a release, but it is beyond his grasp, a timeless existence of good things, of 'playas inmensas como una mirada de amor', of rivers and entwined bodies, where two can unite in the heart of the moment:

> . . . allá el diamante insomne cede
> y en su centro vacío somos el ojo que nunca parpadea y
> la fijeza del instante ensimismado en su esplendor.
>   (*Lib*. 228)

Finally from this vision of a possible paradise the poet is returned once again to face himself in his present time and place. As the walls of the room and the inescapable realities close in once more, there seems to come a realization that only a full acceptance of the moment will bring enlightenment and the perception of that unity in which all being shares:

> aquí es ninguna parte, poco a poco me he ido cerrando y
>   no encuentro salida que no dé a este instante,
> este instante soy yo, salí de pronto de mí mismo, no
>   tengo nombre ni rostro,
> yo está aquí, echado a mis pies, mirándome mirándose
>   mirarme mirado.   (*Lib*. 229)

The moment breaks and the mood changes as the outer world penetrates once more, but now to a changed consciousness, aware of the spiritual rebirth to which suffering can lead:

> Fuera, en los jardines que arrasó el verano, una cigarra
> se ensaña contra la noche.
> ¿Estoy o estuve aquí? (*Lib.* 229)

In 'El río' the river becomes the objective correlative for those things in Nature and in men's lives which are subject to change and motion, that is to the laws of time and space. The course of a life flows like a river, likewise words run successively on to the page to form the poem; in the outside world the life of the city moves onwards with purposeless but inescapable activity. The poet rebels against this ceaseless motion through time and place and asks not for the words of the poem, but for the illumination of poetry—'que las palabras depongan armas y sea el poema una sola palabra entretejida, un resplandor implacable que avanza' (*Lib.* 231). What he is searching for is a vision of eternity, a moment ('un instante') plumbed to its depths and held outside the flow of time:

> Detenerse un instante, detener a mi sangre que va y viene,
> va y viene y no dice nada,
> sentado sobre mí mismo como el yoguín a la sombra de la
> higuera, como Buda a la orilla del río, detener al
> instante,
> un solo instante, sentado a la orilla del tiempo, borrar
> mi imagen del río que habla dormido y no dice nada
> y me lleva consigo,
> sentado a la orilla detener al río, abrir el instante, pene-
> trar por sus salas atónitas hasta su centro de agua,
> beber en la fuente inagotable, ser la cascada de sílabas
> azules que cae de los labios de piedra,
> sentado a la orilla de la noche como Buda a la orilla de
> sí mismo ser el parpadeo del instante . . .
>
> (*Lib.* 230)

Despite the danger of generalizations, the over-all impression left by the collection *Salamandra*, in comparison with earlier and later works, is that of a light obscured. This has been suggested from a different perspective in the previous chapter, in which the surrealist mode is discussed as creating the atmosphere of struggle for emergence from spiritual turmoil, or in mythic terms, for the rebirth to which the travails of initiation ultimately lead. The subtle shifts in usage and meaning which become apparent in Paz's vocabulary in *Salamandra* both support this general theory and show the means by which the change in mood is achieved. The intense moment so often sought and experienced in *Libertad bajo palabra* retreats as the process by which it is achieved becomes correspondingly more painful and less fruitful. The poet accepts less, his mental attitude holds more of doubt and hesitancy than before, and there is less assurance of the possibility of revealed truth.

'Pausa' (*Sal.* 24), written in memory of Pierre Reverdy, is a short, terse poem which moves in few lines from the outer world to the inner state of the poet who is seen as anguished and haunted by the passing of time. Birds fly past, and 'una idea negra' darkens the poet's spirit. Outside he hears sounds of Nature ('Rumor de árboles') and of men ('Rumor de trenes y motores'), and within his consciousness the moment stands still—'¿Va o viene este instante?' The silent glare of the sun penetrates to the heart of sentient beings and inanimate matter, cutting through 'Hasta el grito de piedra de las piedras'. In a complex image the sun, as source of energy, becomes the heart of man, source of life, and together the whole of Nature feeling and suffering—'Sol-corazón, piedra que late'. Yet the suffering is never in vain: 'Piedra de sangre que se vuelve fruto'. The wounds of the heart lie open, but without pain, and the poet's existence merges with all that which time governs: 'Mi vida fluye parecida a la vida.'

'Noche en claro' is a poem grouped around three moments with imperceptible transitions from one to another. Dedicated to André Breton and Benjamin Péret, the occasion of its opening is a café in Paris at ten o'clock on an autumn night. The air is filled with expectancy, both of the gathering mists and of something more, echoed in the thrice-repeated refrain, 'Algo se prepara / Dijo uno entre nosotros'. As the words are repeated for the second time, the expansion of consciousness seems to take place, and the poet sees with clairvoyant eyes:

> Se abrió el minuto en dos
> Leí signos en la frente de este instante . . .
>
> (*Sal.* 60)

The refrain appears again, but 'uno entre nosotros' is now 'el poeta', a change which allows the scene to shift imperceptibly to London. Here a pair in love appear to open a door, as it were, out of the prison of time which 'daba vueltas y vueltas y no pasaba'. The sweethearts' affirmation of love and life gives back identity to the dehumanized puppets into which modern life transforms us, and provides a bridge to a moment of wider vision in which 'Sus luchas sus amores / Son la creación y la destrucción de los mundos . . .' (*Sal.* 62). In this vision 'Parpadea el instante y dice algo' to those who are prepared to hear. The line 'Algo se prepara' returns poet and reader to the scene of the opening. As his friends disappear into the night the poem breaks into a passionate re-affirmation of the truth carried by the lovers—that the self-realization gained through loving acceptance of another human being is universal truth to which the poet bears personal witness.

'Discor' (*Sal.* 96–8) shows the other side of the coin, the imprisonment of the poet in a nightmare present from which he fails to escape. The poem depends upon the mirror-image which is another important motif in Paz's poetry, and thus belongs later in this study. Here, the context in which 'el instante' appears serves well to illustrate the state of mental frustration underlying many of the *Salamandra* poems. The atmosphere of 'Discor' is that of a labyrinthine confusion of spirals, passages, staircases, mirrors which distort or reflect nothing, and rooms full of dismembered bodies and nightmarish apparitions. The poet feels physically captive in space, and in time he is held in a present which denies him refuge in past memories of future expectations. An escape from the passing of time is of course exactly what is sought in moments of transcended consciousness, and is the timelessness of myth, but 'Discor' shows how this process can serve also the powers of darkness to which the human mind is prey. The moment is 'largo como un aullido / Como el presente', and seems metaphorically a staircase which 'No desemboca y siempre desemboca', a tormenting fabrication of a mind in anguish.

To emerge to the spiritual completeness of *Ladera Este* is to be aware almost concretely of the new composure achieved by the poet and communicated through the poems. The blend of Paz's own developing personality with the Brahman and Buddhist metaphysics which awoke so many echoes in his soul produced a more emphatic use of the vocabulary which he has made his own.

Hesitancy has now disappeared displaced by a positive affirmation of personal beliefs. The poet's vision seems two-dimensional: poetry, love, and identification with the rest of being are doorways into a transcending of human limitations, but at the same time they affirm those very limitations. They provide the unified vision which can grasp the human condition in its most ironic paradox—that it *is* tied to the here and now, subject to death and decay, and to the laws of matter. The vision and the understanding which it occasions then turn the gaze of the poet back to the humanity which he accepts as existentially complete in itself, and enable him to make common cause with those who suffer and are wronged. The moments of release become, then, a reaffirmation of the glories of Nature and the vast potential of man himself, precisely because no life beyond death is posited as a final escape. All of man's acceptance and his greatness, or conversely his denial and abjection of the human condition, is pertinent and judged in terms of the existence in which mankind and all being shares. 'Vrindaban' has already been discussed in precisely these terms; the new fullness of meaning which the word 'instante' gains in this context becomes apparent now:

> Sé lo que creo y lo escribo
> Advenimiento del instante
> > > El acto
> El movimiento en que se esculpe
> Y se deshace el ser entero
> Conciencia y manos para asir el tiempo . . .
> > > (*L.E.* 62–3)

It is still the intense moment which the poet shares, but it is also the positive reaching out to time and history which lie behind and are interwoven with our common tradition.

'Tumba del poeta' (*L.E.* 73–5) and 'Carta a León Felipe' (*L.E.* 89–94) seek to involve the reader directly in the experience which has called the poem to the poet's consciousness. 'Tumba del poeta' sets the poet in a metaphysical framework face to face with his tool—language—and his creation—the poem. The instinct of the poet, 'En un allá no sé donde', working through his eyes upon the tangible world around him, leads him to the mystical act of *naming*, of fixing objects 'Con un nombre / Inmortal / Irrisoria corona de espinas / ¡Lenguaje!' This process is at best imperfect, at worst ludicrous, yet always inescapably linked with the deep issues of the nature of reality.[4] Man's tenous bond with both the outer universe and his own inner world is just this arbitrary construction of syllables which constitutes human communication:

> Instantes
> Racimos encendidos
> Selvas andantes de astros
> Sílabas errantes
> Milenios de arena cayendo sin término . . .
>
> (*L.E.* 74)

Yet the poet cannot avoid the burden of the world—his impulse is now 'En un aquí no sé donde', and he is forced to fix with a name, 'Asirlo plantarlo decirlo / . . . Encarnarlo'. As the word is formed the act of creation becomes immediate in time and space— 'Clavado / Como un dios / En este aquí sin donde / ¡Lenguaje!'— and the poem assumes its independent existence: 'Acabo en su comienzo / En esto que digo / Acabo.' The selfhood of the poet retreats into a larger self, and his identity is lost, even to himself:

> SER
> Sombra de un nombre instantáneo
>
> NUNCA SABRÉ MI DESENLACE
>
> (*L.E.* 75)

Once again the mind returns to the young poet in 'Fuente' (*Lib.* 216–18), whose death is required so that poetic truth may live, and further back in time to Alfred de Musset's comparison of the poet with the pelican, who offers his own breast to feed his fledglings:

> Poète, c'est ainsi que font les grands poètes:
> Ils laissent s'égayer ceux qui vivent un temps;
> Mais les festins humains qu'ils servent à leurs fêtes
> Ressemblent la plupart à ceux des pélicans.[5]

It is an image which blends into one of the most basic archetypes of the human consciousness, that of the hero sacrificed to redeem his people.

'Carta a León Felipe' is a more conceptualized meditation upon the function of poetry both as a metaphysical expression and as a live nerve in man's consciousness. Paz explores the paradoxes attendant upon the poet's relations with words and the relations

of words with objects. The poet must 'Aprender a ver oír decir /
Lo instantáneo / . . . ¿*Fijar vértigos?*' He must be a perpetual
conscience, looking beneath the arbitrariness of language and the
hollowness of appearances:

> La poesía
> Es la ruptura instantánea
> Instantáneamente cicatrizada
> Abierta de nuevo
> Por la mirada de los otros
> La ruptura
> Es la continuidad
> La muerte del Comandante Guevara
> También es ruptura
> No un fin
> Su memoria
> No es una cicatriz
> Es una continuidad que se desgarra
> Para continuarse . . .
>
> (*L.E.* 92)

The poet is granted awareness more intense than normal men;
he can glimpse 'el instante', and he has the whole mystical
power of language at his disposal. Yet these impose their own
burden, and *Ladera Este* shows an awareness of responsibilities
on a human plane. The intense moment brings with it now an
enriched experience in the poet who has known growth through
suffering, that is, rebirth through initiation. The dimension of
this rebirth is wide enough to include an acceptance both of
man's existential mortality and of his capacity for spiritual
greatness.

MEDIODÍA

As the intense moment awaited, experienced, and remembered
orders the flow of the poet's life itself into cycles, and as the cycle
of the year moves from the nadir of the winter solstice to the
fullness of summer, so the day has also its rise and decline and its
correspondingly changing atmosphere. Noon is for Paz the magic
moment when time seems suspended or when this suspension
appears most tantalizingly possible. Noon becomes the objective
correlative of the poet's expectancy, the projection upon the
natural cycle of his increased spiritual perceptivity. It is not

surprising therefore that noon plays its largest role in Paz's poetic trajectory in the earliest of his three volumes. *Salamandra* is not the place to look for anticipation and confidence, and *Ladera Este* shows a man whose maturity has lessened his dependence upon outer phenomena and also his dependence as poet upon images and symbols.

Nevertheless, the motif of noon is important in the total structure of Paz's *œuvre*. It carries with it connotations of the supernatural, in that noon for the ancients was the time when phantoms appear, and when the soul was in its greatest peril.[6] The horror of the portents in Shakespeare's *Julius Caesar* is heightened by the time of day at which they are seen:

> And yesterday the bird of night did sit,
> Even at noon-day, upon the market-place,
> Hooting and shrieking.
>
> (Act I, sc. ii)

In the physical context of Paz's Mexican background, noon marks the time when the sun casts its most diaphanous light, after the early freshness of the morning and before the torrid afternoon. In his spiritual world it represents the moment when the visible and invisible spheres of reality most nearly coincide, so that the day can go either way, opening up to the moment of unified vision or to the maleficent powers of the darker side of existence.

One of the earliest poems of *Libertad bajo palabra*, the first 'Soneto' of 1935 (*Lib.* 14), expresses the ambiguous quality of this moment:

> Luz que no se derrama, ya diamante,
> detenido esplendor del mediodía,
> sol que no se consume ni se enfría
> de cenizas y fuego equidistante.

The poem 'El pájaro' of 1944 (*Lib.* 41) resolves this ambiguity with the sharp song of a bird which translates itself in the poet's mind to a dark reflection upon death. The bird's song comes like a 'delgada flecha' to cut across the 'silencio transparente' of the empty day suspended in moments drawn out to the utmost. It is the waiting time of noon:

> En la quietud absorta
> se consumaba el mediodía

The quietude of Nature is shattered by the bird, and that of the poet's mind by the intuition this brings:

> Y sentí que la muerte era una flecha
> que no se sabe quién dispara
> y en un abrir los ojos nos morimos.

In the light of the paradox of the last line the bird's song becomes an objective correlative for the ultimate awareness which can flash through the mind only at the moment when the darkness of death closes in.

Noon and the bird appear again in the series of haiku called 'En Uxmal' (*Lib*. 142-3) which appeared in *Piedras sueltas* of 1955. In this later poem Paz has made use of the same elements and the same atmosphere, almost the same word ('El tiempo en el minuto se saciaba' of 'El pájaro', and 'el tiempo se vacía de minutos' of 'En Uxmal'). But the tone of the haiku is restrained, and what the earlier poem says, this only suggests:

> La luz no parpadea
> el tiempo se vacía de minutos,
> se ha detenido un pájaro en el aire.
>   (*Lib*. 142)

Furthermore, since it is written in the present tense, while 'El pájaro' retells a remembered scene and a remembered reflection, the haiku, true to its form, presents the scene to the reader with the barest of outlines. Then it withdraws, allowing poetic suggestiveness to work as it may. Not only is the contrast between these two poems interesting *per se*, it also shows in miniature the movement of Paz's poetry towards increasing terseness of statement and many more demands that the reader provide the receptive energy needed to complement that of the creative moment.

Two early poems, 'Mediodía' (*Lib*. 34-5) and 'Medianoche' (*Lib*. 38-9), start from the motif of noon with the connotations which it now carries from poet to reader, and relate its particular atmosphere intimately to the poet's personal states of mind and body. 'Mediodía' describes the poet's feeling of merging with the oneness of Nature through the agency of the sun's light and the deepening shadows. Its ending shows that in a world of opposites, these are blended in a wholeness which the poetic vision allows us to see:

Medianoche del cuerpo, toda cielo,
bosque de pulsaciones y espesura,
nocturno mediodía del subsuelo,

¿este caer en una entraña oscura
es de la misma luz del mediodía
que erige lo que toca en escultura?

— El cuerpo es infinito y melodía.

(*Lib.* 35)

Likewise 'Medianoche' explores the intuitions which reach the poet's soul at midnight, a moment which becomes akin to the visionary time of noon:

Es el secreto mediodía.
El alma canta, cara al cielo,
y sueña en otro canto,
sólo vibrante luz,
plenitud silenciosa de lo vivo.

(*Lib.* 39)

The collection of surrealist prose poems, ¿ *Aguila o sol?* (*Lib.* 145–207), contains the noon motif three times, in very different contexts, but with an underlying unity of meaning. 'Llano' (*Lib.* 191) sets up a scene in which human activity becomes equated with the ceaseless motion of insects: the ant-hill is overflowing with bubbling commotion, children and dogs poke among garbage. In a church the statue of a saint is alive with a stream of insects flying constantly between its left eye and the cupola; outside, factories, like decapitated phalli, are filled with human insects working. Over all this the sun 'hunde sus picas en las jarobas del llano'. The poet forces himself to gigantic efforts, fighting through 'grandes rocas de años . . . corredores que se cierran como labios de granito', attempting, perhaps, to escape this scene where energy seems doomed by its own futility. What he finds to counterbalance this frenzy is the impersonal plain and the magic moment of noon, not offering escape or transcendence, but fixed in a perpetual present which is itself a timelessness: 'Y vuelve al llano, al llano donde siempre es mediodía, donde un sol idéntico cae fijamente sobre un paisaje detenido. Y no acaban de caer las doce campanadas, ni de zumbar las moscas,

ni de estallar en astillas este minuto que no pasa, que sólo arde y
no pasa' (*Lib.* 191). The final impression is like that left by much
of Paz's surrealist writing: that of a search for rebirth acknowledged
yet unrewarded, as though the spiritual sterility itself were one of
the labours through which the aspiring soul must pass to deserve
the expansion of consciousness for which it is striving. The fixity
of noon on the plain is an incompleted promise in 'Llano', but
in the over-all pattern of the poet's developing vision it has its
place.

'Mariposa de obsidiana' (*Lib.* 193–5) personifies the native
soul of Mexico, submerged by the Spanish conquest, but sur-
viving in the destiny of the country and its people. Paz's footnote
explains that he is referring to '*Itzpapálotl*, diosa a veces confundida
con *Teteoinan*, nuestra madre, y *Tonatzin*. Todas estas divinidades
femeninas se han fundido en el culto que desde el siglo XVI se
profesa a la Virgen de Guadalupe' (*Lib.* 193). The goddess herself
sings the lament for her past glory and her present desolation.
She was once the eternal feminine in all its aspects, symbolizing
all things to all men: 'Yo era el mediodía tatuado y la medianoche
desnuda, el pequeño insecto de jade que canta entre las yerbas
del amanecer y el zenzontle de barro que convoca a los muertos'
(*Lib.* 194). Noon is then that fullest moment of potential life
when man's reach and grasp are most likely, if ever, to coincide.
This concept carries through to the series of aphorisms, 'Hacia el
poema' (*Lib.* 205–7), which ends *¿Aguila o sol?* Here the poet
sees the function of the poem as a path to transcendence for all
humanity, where a new awareness of man as social and as metaphysical being will be found:

> *Mediodía futuro, árbol inmenso de follaje invisible. En las plazas cantan
> los hombres y las mujeres el canto solar, surtidor de transparencias. Me
> cubre la marejada amarilla: nada mío ha de hablar por mi boca.*

The moment of vision is metaphorically represented as noon for
those who have struggled to emerge from darkness.

And so it is that at this transcendental moment motifs inter-
twine, and linguistic intensity matches that of theme. In 'Himno
entre ruinas' (*Lib.* 211–13), for instance, despite the paradoxes of
human behaviour which cannot be ignored even when the beauty
of external reality produces personal illumination, the final note
is one of exhilarated break-through:

Como el coral sus ramas en el agua
extiendo mis sentidos en la hora viva:
el instante se cumple en una concordancia amarilla,
¡oh mediodía, espiga henchida de minutos,
copa de eternidad!

(*Lib.* 212–13)

The 'instante', the intense moment in Paz's world, is of course
noon, and it is then that the mirror-prison of the human image
shatters as in 'Fuente':

... la presencia, el presente, estalla
como un espejo roto al mediodía, como un mediodía roto
contra el mar y la sal.

(*Lib.* 217)

After *Libertad bajo palabra* the noon motif recurs less often.
Yet in 'Vaivén' (*Sal.* 83–5) its appearance coincides with a return
to Paz's conviction that sexual love is one of the legitimate rites
of passage to a state of higher consciousness. Just as the intense
moment comes to him often through the losing of self in passion,
so this poem, lyricizing the union of lover and beloved, uses
the symbolism of noon to describe the passing from the limitations
of the individual body into union:

Hoy que se abre y se cierra
Nunca se mueve y no se detiene
Corazón que nunca se apaga
Hoy (un pájaro se posa
En una torre de granizo)
Siempre es mediodía

(*Sal.* 85)

Twice in *Ladera Este* the faculty of memory introduces the
noon motif, suggesting perhaps that in his mature years the poet
has become aware of the role of memory in delineating and pre-
serving the precious moments of insight. 'El balcón' (*L.E.* 11–16)
embodies the reflections of the poet who stands at night on a
balcony overlooking Delhi. He is questioning the reality of the
city around him and with it his own identity, the paradox of
his bodily presence in time and space, and the timeless reality of his
mind and spirit. Early in the complex transitions of the poem he
becomes aware that past memories can sometimes carry more

reality for him than present surroundings, and he describes the visionary moment which is now occupying his mind:

> (Trono de hueso
>   Trono del mediodía
> Aquella isla
>   En su cantil leonado
> Por un instante vi la vida verdadera
> Tenía la cara de la muerte
> Eran el mismo rostro
>   Disuelto
> En el mismo mar centelleante)
>   (*L.E.* 12–13)

Noon again symbolizes a moment of perception, though the vision is one of death—not death as the negation of and end to life, but rather as the other half of the life principle which it complements and fulfils. This understanding of life and death as two manifestations of the same principle of universal being may well be one of the profoundest truths arrived at in Paz's poetry, in mythic terms the prize won after initiation, spiritually the emergence into expanded consciousness.

In 'Vrindaban' (*L.E.* 57–63) the Hindu holy man gazes out from his 'interminable mediodía' of which he has chosen to communicate (and thus share) nothing. The poet realizes by contrast that his own justification for existence lies precisely in his being 'Conciencia y manos para asir el tiempo / . . . Una memoria que se inventa' (*L.E.* 63). His task is to point the way ('A oscuras voy y planto signos'), and memory provides its fund of illuminated moments:

> (Escribo
> Cada letra es un germen
>   La memoria
> Insiste en su marea
> Y repite su mismo mediodía)
>   (*L.E.* 61)

The motifs of 'el instante' and 'mediodía' recur so often in Paz's poetry that they provide valid examples of this semiotic mode, which develops themes of great profundity through basic images capable of greater or lesser expansion according to the experience which is being translated into the poem. The conception basic to the use of these words is Paz's conviction that these are moments of vision which human beings can perceive and which constitute a rebirth on a higher spiritual plane. Memory finally enters as a repository for past intuitions which cannot be lost entirely but are kept in the mind.[7] There they provide a basis for belief in their own validity and faith in the liberating processes, seen by Paz as living, loving, and creating.

ESPEJO

Naturally enough, if noon and 'el instante' mark the moments of transcendence of the human condition, the soul which knows them will have to face the reality of their absence. The contrast between those occasions when the door is opened and those when it is closed provides the tension of opposites from which alone, according to Jung, energy proceeds.[8] The noon motif, associated with diaphanous light and a transparent atmosphere, is counterbalanced by the motif of the mirror. This in general terms represents the world of appearances when we are imprisoned within it and the moment of enlightenment is denied. Paz's use of the word 'espejo' follows, in incidence and nuance, a similar trajectory to his use of 'mediodía', though of course with opposite effects. In the earlier portions of *Libertad bajo palabra* the image often appears, but carries a vaguer meaning than in the mature poems of *¿Aguila o sol?* (*Lib.* 146–207) and *La estación violenta* (*Lib.* 211–54). In these its meaning crystallizes into that of present reality, spatial or temporal, which mocks the explorer seeking to escape, by reflecting a distortion of his own face, or worse, nothing at all. The mirror can be shattered, however, and light re-enter the world of the mind, as the poems of *La estación violenta* make apparent. *Salamandra* picks up the frustrating and imprisoning effects of the mirror-image, and the breaking of its reflection is forgotten in the anguish which its existence produces. Its horror has been lost in *Ladera Este*, however, and its reappearance becomes more a linguistic formality in the sense that the growth of the poet's personal vocabulary persists, though the individual signs fluctuate in the amount and quality of the meaning which they carry. The signs themselves give linguistic unity to the whole, but the significance of each can expand and contract according to the new experience which the artist wishes to communicate.

A poem dated 1934 and entitled 'Espejo' (*Lib.* 55–6) re-creates
a mood of alienation when the poet tries to explore the reality of
his own existence and the nature of his solitude. The first stanza
creates a general atmosphere of desolation both in time and in
space. There is no comfort for the anguished mind; time is
hollow ('hueco'), or full of horrors ('una noche de uñas y
silencio'), and the world in which the speaker stands alone is a
'páramo sin orillas, / isla de yelo entre los días . . .' (*Lib.* 55).
The second stanza introduces the figure of the poet returning
to this nightmare from which no human contact, even the sweet-
ness of passion, can release him. He cannot evade the issue of
his own identity, yet the mirrors around him merely reflect back
the 'persona' through which not even he can reach the true self:

> Y entre espejos impávidos un rostro
> me repite a mi rostro, un rostro
> que enmascara a mi rostro.
>
> (*Lib.* 56)

The seeming reality of outer appearances becomes meaningless
to him who can find no core inside himself. Stanza three sets the
'juegos fatuos del espejo' against the paradoxical existence of the
poet in whose being layer after layer of conflicting identities deny
each other to the 'yo penúltimo, / que sólo pide olvido, sombra,
nada, / final mentira que lo enciende y quema'. The mirror reveals
only the lying mask of visible reality, yet even the most caustic
introspection cannot pierce the ultimate mask. In the un-
certainty of his own identity the poem ends:

> De una máscara a otra
> hay siempre un yo penúltimo que pide.
> Y me hundo en mí mismo y no me toco.
>
> (*Lib.* 56)

'Ni el cielo ni la tierra' (*Lib.* 58–9) expresses a violent loss of
faith in previously accepted values both human and divine, and
extends the mirror motif accordingly. This appears twice in the
poem, not now as merely a neutral or mocking agent, but with
maleficent overtones. The poet denounces heaven and the futility
of earth along with his own physical being:

> Atrás mi piel de vidrios erizados,
> atrás mis uñas y mis dientes
> caídos en el pozo del espejo.
>
> (*Lib.* 58)

Human love has failed him, and the organized Church seems worse than hypocritical in the empty sham which destroys the poor it should help. Religion is a broken mirror, not one which shatters to reveal transcendent truths, but one which deceives even Narcissus, led by vanity to seek sustenance there:

> — la Sagrada Familia en su Pesebre,
> la Fuente de la Vida,
> el espejo quebrado en que Narciso
> a sí mismo se bebe y no se sacia . . .
>
> (*Lib.* 59)

Nothing remains of former beliefs now that there is no consolation in deception—even the fountain of life where previously the seeker found at least himself has been shown up as a delusion. Only sorrow remains: 'También el llanto sirve de almohada.'

The tone of 'La vida sencilla' (*Lib.* 78–9) is that of desperation overcome in resignation, and of human imperfections accepted with dignity. The poem is less an affirmation of this resignation and this dignity achieved, however, than an appeal for these qualities, as the 'envío' makes clear. In this new context the mirror becomes a witness of reality which must be faced with courage and on its own terms—appearances cannot logically show more than what is on the surface, but that surface can be worthy of itself:

> probar la soledad sin que el vinagre
> haga torcer mi boca, ni repita
> mis muecas el espejo, ni el silencio
> se erice con los dientes que rechinan . . .
>
> (*Lib.* 78–9)

In the solitude of which Paz's earlier work is constantly aware, the mirror is a symbol of that outer reality which may not be escaped. It must be reckoned with on its own terms, for it will never lead to the truths which lie within and will hideously distort whatever inner longings place themselves at its mercy. This much an example from 'El ausente' (*Lib.* 94–7) will corroborate. The poet searches in vain for God and cannot find proof even of his own identity in the mirror:

> Alguna vez, frente a frente yo mismo,
> se deshizo mi rostro en el espejo:
> ¿eras mi propio rostro,
> ese helado reflejo de la nada?
>
> (*Lib.* 96)

The mirror motif appears also in several poems which concern the poet's relation with language. In the early poem 'Palabra' (*Lib.* 31) the word is 'herida y fuente: espejo; / espejo y resplendor . . .', one of the simpler uses of the motif as merely the reflection in the word of the poet's experience. A more complex image is created in 'Fábula' (*Lib.* 121–2), again with the broken mirror which, as in 'Ni el cielo ni la tierra', has connotations of a paradise lost. 'Fábula' joins the union known in love with visions of an earlier, mystical unity of existence in a lost age of bliss:

> Todo era de todos
> > Todos eran todo
> Solo había una palabra inmensa y sin revés
> Palabra como un sol . . .
>
> > > (*Lib.* 122)

Disharmony entered this undifferentiated world and with it language, the discursive fragments of a lost unity:

> Un día se rompió en fragmentos diminutos
> Son las palabras del lenguaje que hablamos
> Fragmentos que nunca se unirán
> Espejos rotos donde el mundo se mira destrozado . . .
>
> > > (*Lib.* 122)

Thus the mirror motif acts as one of the threads unifying Paz's great themes of epistemology, solitude, and language.

It would be impractical and undesirable to catalogue all the appearances of the mirror in Paz's poetry. But it is important to note the more precise significance which it develops in *¿Aguila o sol?* and *La estación violenta*. The mirror begins to carry more definitely the overtone of imprisonment, both in time, in space, and in self, which is of course the same thing. 'La higuera' (*Lib.* 195–6) describes the poet's boyhood in Mixcoac and the strange presence which the fig-tree held for him. His days there were lonely, shut-in days, and the mirror, interpreted as selfhood, is one of the obstacles to his freedom:

Encerrado en cuatro muros (al norte el cristal del no saber, paisaje por inventar; al sur, la memoria cuarteada; al este, el espejo; al oeste, la cal y el canto del silencio) . . .

> > > (*Lib.* 195)

Imprisonment in time is described in 'El sitiado' (*Lib.* 203), in which the poet is trapped in the no man's land between moments of inspiration when time is turned in upon him:[9] 'Horas relucientes, espejos pulidos por la espera . . .' If such incarceration is to be overcome, the mirror of selfhood must be broken, as 'Himno entre ruinas' (*Lib.* 211–13) describes in its final stanza. This brings reader and poet through the shades of the underworld into a visionary light:

> La inteligencia al fin encarna,
> se reconcilian las dos mitades enemigas
> y la conciencia-espejo se licúa,
> vuelve a ser fuente, manantial de fábulas:
> Hombre, árbol de imágenes,
> palabras que son flores que son frutos que son actos.
>
> (*Lib.* 213)

The great poems which follow, 'Fuente', 'Repaso nocturno', 'Mutra', 'Piedra de sol', all provide examples of this transition to a higher plane of awareness once the mirror of fruitless selfhood has been demolished. One final example of the importance of the motif at this stage of Paz's work may be drawn from 'Máscaras del alba' (*Lib.* 213–16), written in Venice in 1948 and taking dawn over St. Mark's Square as its starting-point. The second stanza uses the mirror-image in a complex interior duplication as the dying man catches the first glimpse of the coming dawn. The early light and the promise of the sun are objective correlatives for another light which will soon be his in death. For death comes as the final reality in which all else dissolves, the ultimate mirror of mirrors, being itself which unifies all perspectives and in which all the distorted images of our partial reality are resolved:

> Abre los ojos el agonizante.
> Esa brizna de luz que tras cortinas
> espía al que la expía entre estertores
> es la mirada que no mira y mira,
> el ojo en que espejean las imágenes
> antes de despeñarse, el precipicio
> cristalino, la tumba de diamante:
> es el espejo que devora espejos.
>
> (*Lib.* 214)

When the motif reappears in *Salamandra* it is not accompanied by any feeling of relief through the shattering of the mirror. It carries at every appearance the sense of imprisonment which the general mood of the *Salamandra* poems would lead the reader to expect. 'Repeticiones' (*Sal.* 15–16) is one of the most hopeless expressions of all Paz's work. Human life is suffered as a futile round of meaningless gestures, at best empty, at worst menacing. In the poet's underworld wanderings in search of rebirth, this is among the moments of greatest horror. All the normal functions of living are reduced to empty formalities, with the motif 'Camino andado / camino desandado' appearing five times to emphasize the pointlessness of existence which goes nowhere but back upon itself. As is often the case in *Salamandra*, the man-made mechanisms of city life add to the desolation of the poet's spiritual state. And the mirror appears as silent accuser of man's guilt, undeserved but unavoidable, and in the context of this poem inescapable:

> El laberinto de la culpa sin culpa
> El espejo que recrimina y el silencio que rasguña
> El día estéril la noche estéril el dolor estéril . . .
>
> (*Sal.* 16)

The world has become a waiting-room where no one waits, a road 'andado y desandado', and life moves on impassive to man's pain.

It is possible to make an interesting comparison of two identical images based on the mirror motif to show how wide the associative field of a given word may be. One of the metaphors in most danger of becoming a cliché is that which associates mirrors with eyes. Paz himself does this twice, and the difference in tone between the two occasions shows how subtle a psychological link exists between the 'name' and the 'sense', and how great a fluctuation there may be in the latter.[10] 'Tus ojos' (*Lib.* 113) expresses the paradoxical images called up in the poet by the eyes of the beloved. The paradoxes ('silencio que habla / tempestades sin viento, mar sin olas') are not presented as though to build up an experience of some ineffable truth; they seem more to explore the *anima* principle in life, at the same time creative and destructive—the Kali–Devi dichotomy—and the tone of the poem is more that of surprised discovery than revelation. The woman's eyes, in fact, contain for the poet all aspects of reality. They mirror the visible world and also show the way to another plane of existence, the important point being that the first image does not at this juncture exclude the second: 'espejos de este mundo, puertas del más allá.' 'Noche en claro' (*Sal.* 59–64) is one of the poems in that volume in which alienation is transcended in the moment of vision. Yet the mirror motif is now associated clearly with the awareness of self which does not allow that moment to come to so many of the spiritually blind. The poet describes the dehumanization of the city, this time in London, and the unseeing eyes around him are not only mirrors through which no inner life can be perceived, but blinded mirrors, annulling even outer reality:

> Nadie tenía cara aquella tarde
> En el underground de Londres
> En lugar de ojos
>   Abominación de espejos cegados . . .
>   (*Sal.* 60)

It is precisely this combination of developing 'sense' and unchanging 'name' which allows discussion of a semiotic mode in Paz's poetry. The recurrence of motifs early on creates in the reader an affective response to the meaning which these carry, and this response is able to grasp in full perspective the evolving 'sense' which the now familiar 'name' carries.

The last notable example of the mirror motif in *Salamandra* is 'Discor' (*Sal.* 96–8), which is focused almost entirely upon this image. In 'Discor' the mirror again combines imprisonment in space and in time, but with the emphasis on the latter, so that the mirror-image now expands to include the sense of an oppressive, inescapable present. The poem is a poem of lovers, but not even love is here able to break through the nightmare of life as it haunts the poet's mind. It is as though a lovely melody attempts to be heard within a cacophony of sound which finally absorbs it. The sounds of this cacophony are images isolated, discordant, and recurrent: the staircase which 'no desemboca y siempre desemboca' the 'espiral indecisa', the 'gastados carmesíes', and especially the mirror. This first of all distorts the relationship between the two lovers, 'Otra tú misma que no me conoce / Y tú reconoces', and then becomes part of the nightmare of an inescapable present, as the feeling of passing time disappears:

> Abolición del tiempo
> Espejo llagado y llaga perpetua . . .
>   (*Sal.* 96)

As the lovers try to combat this sensation with the warmth of passion, the body too ceases to have reality, and the relationship between the girl and her own self is distorted along with all around them:

> Abolición del cuerpo
> Otra tú misma que tú no conoces
> Nace del espejo abolido . . .
> (*Sal.* 97)

The mirrors not only alienate what is reflected in them, but they also multiply: 'Fornicación espectral de los espejos . . .' They threaten all reality by freezing time in a hideous present: 'Los espejos engendran / Fijo presente que sale al encuentro . . .' The lovers have no power to restore harmony; they can only flee from their false images and lose themselves in a night which the mirrors hold in the menace of an inflexible present.

The 'sense' of the mirror motif contracts in *Ladera Este*. Thematically it is almost redundant in poems where a corresponding expansion of meaning accrues to an image such as 'la otra orilla', with its transcendental connotations. The mirror seems to have been broken for Paz himself after 'Discor', and it can now leave the outer edges of its associative field and return to its more literal centre of meaning. It is still a part of Paz's vocabulary; it is still drawn on imagistically, but its evil threats have been exorcized, and it provides a harmless element in descriptions such as that in 'Maithuna':

> Hora vertical
> La sequía
> Mueve sus ruedas espejeantes . . .
> (*L.E.* 117)

It comes to the poet's mind in his parting remembrance of Delhi in 'Cuento de dos jardines':

> Arquitecturas sin peso,
>   Cristalizaciones
> Casi mentales,
>   Altos vértigos sobre un espejo.
>   (*L.E.* 141)

But the best summary of its infrequency in this volume is the last line of this same poem, 'Los signos se borran: yo miro la claridad', which metaphorically expresses the very rebirth from the agonizing mirror world which 'Discor' sought and failed to find.

TRANSPARENCIA[11]

The desire for or experience of transparent light provides one of the most personal motifs in Paz's poetry. It expresses so basic an element in his beliefs, both metaphysical and poetic, if the two can be separated in his case, that it is equally evident in all three volumes. Paz's world of rebirth is one of diaphanous clarity, the intense moment in time being matched by a lifting of the normal density of the atmosphere. Spiritual awareness is accompanied by increased sensual perceptions of which the most obvious is that of vision, as light of a new quality descends upon the scene and the poet's senses.

That the prime inspiration for this awareness of the quality of light is the sun of Mexico seems obvious. Its importance in Paz's poetic world is paramount and not coincidental. It is difficult to visualize, for instance, this sun-drenched light as a vital element in the poetry of any English poet as dependent upon native tradition as is Paz. There are exceptions, of course, such as D. H. Lawrence, who followed the sun because it was essential to his inspiration. Yet normally so strong an awareness of sun and light comes from the artist's roots in the soil. *¿Aguila o sol?* provides many instances where the poet explores his relation with his country. 'Valle de México' (*Lib.* 202) opens with the line 'El día despliega su cuerpo transparente', and continues with images of sunlight so strong that it vibrates and dazzles. 'El sitiado' (*Lib.* 203) also opens with descriptions of time and place (the latter Mexico): 'A mi izquierda el verano despliega sus verdes libertades, sus claros y cimas de ventura: follajes, transparencias . . . Zumba el sol.'

From this literal starting-point concentric circles of metaphoric significance spread out around the word. The line 'Voy entre transparencias' ('Arcos', *Lib.* 35) describes that translucid moment before the experience of the poem takes shape in words; silence as well as light can assume the promise with which transparency seems associated:

> En el silencio transparente
> el día reposaba:

la transparencia del espacio
era la transparencia del silencio.
('El pájaro', *Lib.* 41)

In the moment of vision it becomes synonymous with the inner
essence of things:

y para dar respuesta a mis atónitas preguntas
el fuego se hacía humo
el árbol temblor de hojas, el agua transparencia . . .
('Soliloquio de medianoche', *Lib.* 100)

Language itself, if it is to regain the power which has been lost
through years of misuse, must become transparent: 'Y tú, viento
que soplas del Pasado, sopla con fuerza, dispersa estas pocas
sílabas y hazlas aire y transparencia . . .' ('Los trabajos del poeta',
Lib. 158). And again, from 'Erlaban' (*Lib.* 189), 'Allá el lenguaje
consiste en la producción de objetos hermosos y transparentes . . .'

The great poems of *La estación violenta* and 'Piedra de sol'
use 'transparency' in its most transcendent sense. In a passage
already quoted from 'Hacia el poema' the intense moment
objectified as noon is directly connected with the arrival of a new
lucidity of vision: '*Mediodía futuro, árbol inmenso de follaje invisible.
En las plazas cantan los hombres y las mujeres el canto solar, surtidor
de transparencias*' (*Lib.* 207). In 'El río', transparency is a quality
which Nature assumes in the mystic moment to which the whole
poem tends:

y sea todo como la llama que se esculpe y se
hiela en la roca de entrañas transparentes,
duro fulgor resuelto ya en cristal y claridad
pacífica.
(*Lib.* 232)

But the most open declaration of this moment appears in 'Piedra
de sol', where the motif of 'transparencia' assumes its most
elevated sense:

el mundo se despoja de sus máscaras
y en su centro, vibrante transparencia,
lo que llamamos Dios . . .
(*Lib.* 249)

Even amid the existential suffering of much of *Salamandra* the
motif does not disappear. There is a retrenchment in the meaning

which it carries, but it does not diminish in frequency. For Paz
there is obviously always a lamp, or the memory of one, even in
darkness.

Of all the appearances of the transparency motif in *Salamandra*,
'El tiempo mismo' (39–45) is the most fruitful for considering
the semiotic mode, as it combines the dual preoccupations of
Paz, that is reality and language. In the poem's double trajectory
two moments of insight are reached, both of which culminate
in a translucence of air and of mood. The poem opens in the city,
the sounds of Nature are unnaturally replaced by the silence of
that man-made entity, 'Perdida en su propia inmensidad / Sin
alcanzarse nunca / Ni poder salir de sí misma' (*Sal.* 39). The
poet's thoughts of life and death are interrupted by the sight of an
old man on a bench and a pair of lovers, but he returns to the
contrast between daily motion and the inner awareness of life
which men often neglect or take for granted. At this point, in the
silence of the night and his own being, language crystallizes for
him into a poem, and he realizes that he writes to make time live
for him ('para que me viva'):

> Arquitectos de silencio
> Y de pronto sin más porque sí
> La palabra
>   Alabastro
> Esbelta transparencia no llamada
> Haría música con ella
>   Castillos en el aire . . .
>   (*Sal.* 41–2)

Time then becomes the point of his questioning, and as he gazes
upon the beauty of outer reality which seems outside the dimension
of temporality, it seems to him that time and beauty are one and
the same, so that man might measure his life by beauty instead of
by time. What his insight tells him is that only the shadow of
time passes, that time itself is suspended in 'las presencias', 'Lo
presente sentido', which the sight of a blackbird, 'Negro / Centro
de claridades', can communicate to us. Within the passage of
time there is another essential time which man can only intuit but
which, because it is eternal, gives reality to the life of the spirit:

> Dentro del tiempo hay otro tiempo
> Quieto
>   Sin horas ni peso ni sombra

> Sin pasado o futuro
> Sólo vivo
> Como el viejo del banco
> Unimismado idéntico perpetuo
> Nunca lo vemos Es la transparencia
> (*Sal.* 45)

Although the transparency motif reappears with equal frequency throughout *Ladera Este*, it does not acquire any expansion of meaning. Perhaps no further expansion is possible, since there must somewhere be a limit to the development of the 'sense' of every 'name'. Having adopted the connotation of essential reality, the image of translucent light can expand no further. It continues to illuminate Paz's inner and outer world, however, so that the recent poetry no less than the earlier creates an aura of diaphanous clarity associated with the transcendence brought to this poet by love and poetry and the intuition of life itself. In 'Contigo' (*L.E.* 113) the intense experience of the day and of the loved woman produces in the poet a moment of synthesis in which life and death are understood as complementary halves of the same reality, and this moment is one of transparent light:

> Soy real
> Veo mi vida y mi muerte
> El mundo es verdadero
> Veo
> Habito una transparencia.

'Tumba del poeta' (*L.E.* 73–5) objectifies an inner vision with a lifting of the light on the horizon in an 'Extensión inmaculada / Transparencia que sostiene a las cosas'. In 'Viento entero' (*L.E.* 101–8) the moment of meeting a girl transforms time and all external reality in the poet's eyes:

> La muchacha real
> Transparencia del mundo
> El presente es perpetuo . . .
> (*L.E.* 104)

Of many other examples, 'Cuento de dos jardines' provides a fitting conclusion in its last few lines. The experiences which have centred around the two gardens have been communicated, and the poet is sailing away from the continent where the second garden was. The land behind him is disappearing in brilliant light,

'Espiral de transparencias', and at the same time the garden in his mind is transformed from a place into an identity without name or substance. It has been reduced to its essence; the objectification of this essence as a spiral of transparencies catches imagistically the ultimate meaning of 'transparencia' within Paz's personal vocabulary.

PRESENCIA

It begins to seem almost tautological to insist that these moments of break-through which give to Paz's poetry so clearly the form of the life–death–rebirth cycle are accompanied by awareness of some extraterrestrial presence. From all that has gone before this is obviously so. Yet a discussion of Paz's semiotic mode must insist upon this point by exploring the variations of 'sense' which lie behind the 'name', 'presencia' in his poetry.

The first evident fact about this concept is its relationship with the *anima* principle. From first to last, no matter what expansion of meaning it may undergo, the sense of the ineffable presence is felt through the body of a loved woman. Not exclusively so, for there is an expansion of meaning which covers at times a whole awareness of the eternal cosmic principle, but the motif of 'presencia' as *anima* is one of the most important unifiers of Paz's work. 'Raíz del hombre' (*Lib.* 24–6) provides an early example, here in its simplest form. The feeling of a presence is projected upon the being of the beloved with few overtones beyond the affective:

> No hay vida o muerte
> tan sólo tu presencia,
> inundando los tiempos,
> destruyendo mi ser y su memoria.
> (*Lib.* 26)

Yet even here the reader is aware of an upsurge of unconscious dreams and impulses which allows the conscious ego to be submerged in a timeless existence beyond the reaches of memory. Through the presence embodied in the woman the personal identity is lost in a collective existence at an unconscious level.

This basic meaning of 'presencia' continues. 'Otoño' (*Lib.* 53–4) is the search for some source of comfort, 'unas manos, / una presencia, un cuerpo'. The first encounter with the loved one in

'Piedra de sol' appears as 'una presencia como un canto súbito' (*Lib.* 237); in 'Noche en claro' (*Sal.* 59–64) the poet is overwhelmed by the feeling of a presence in which his awareness of the city as a living entity blends with the unconscious force tying him to the loved woman. His consciousness merges both images until the city, the woman, and the mysterious presence are all one: 'Ciudad o Mujer Presencia' becomes 'Ciudad Mujer Presencia' in the final insight. The terror which the force of the *anima* inspires becomes part of the vision of 'Noche en claro':

> Aquí la belleza no es legible
> Aquí la presencia se vuelve terrible . . .
> *(Sal.* 63)

The ties which the poet feels binding him to this awful presence merge into a cosmic vision which becomes the timelessness of myth, or of eternity:

> Aquí la estrella es negra
> La luz es sombra luz la sombra
> Aquí el tiempo se para
> Los cuatro puntos cardinales se tocan . . .
> *(Sal.* 64)

The return to reality can take place only as all time becomes that of the encounter with the woman, and all space focuses on the 'lugar solitario el lugar de la cita'. Through the *anima* felt as 'Ciudad Mujer Presencia' the poet's unconscious and conscious selves regain harmony and time once more becomes a reality: 'Aquí comienza el tiempo.'

'Carta a León Felipe' (*L.E.* 89–94) includes a very matter-of-fact statement of this same awareness of the mysterious feminine principle through a woman's body:

> El cuerpo femenino
> 　　　　　　Es una pausa
> 　Terrible
> 　　　　Proximidad inaccesible
> La demasía de la presencia
> 　　　　　　　　Fija
> Y no obstante
> 　　　　Desbordante . . .
> *(L.E.* 93)

The intuitive experience of the same feeling appears in 'Viento entero' (*L.E.* 102–8) when the poet and the girl first meet:

> Una muchacha real
> Entre las casas y las gentes espectrales
> Presencia chorro de evidencias . . .
> (*L.E.* 102)

From this central concept of presence as *anima*, the poet allows the word to acquire wider meanings, including more of the archetypal urgings of the unconscious, even the god-urge itself.[12] 'Cerca del cabo Camorín' (*L.E.* 43–4) describes a landscape transfigured in the poet's mood of illumination. Here the surrounding presence is felt through all of Nature as an enveloping, life-giving force:

> Y la invisible,
> Aunque constante, pánica presencia . . .
> (*L.E.* 43)

There are other examples which show how the power of the natural cycle is connected in the poet's spirit with the emergence of the presence: from 'Mutra' (*Lib.* 222), 'este día y las presencias que alza o derriba el sol con un simple aletazo'; from 'Un día de tantos' (*Sal.* 69–70), 'Antes de irse / El sol incendia las presencias'. 'Utacamud' (*L.E.* 41–2) arrives through different perspectives of Indian scenery to a presence which is impenetrable and inexpressible, 'Indiferente al vértigo — y al lenguaje'.

The presence brings with it an awareness of timelessness, since the collective unconscious from which it comes exists in a sphere outside history or memory. In an early poem, 'Junio' (*Lib.* 37), it is explicitly stated: 'Hora de eternidad, toda presencia . . .' Even more powerful is the later 'Fuente' (*Lib.* 216–18), in which the moment is being prepared for the sacrifice of the poet-victim:

> Todo es presencia, todos los siglos son este Presente
> ¡Ojo feliz que ya no mira porque todo es presencia
> y su propia visión fuera de sí lo mira!
> (*Lib.* 217)

This timelessness is expressed in 'El tiempo mismo' (*Sal.* 39–45) as the essence within time itself and outside its domain, as there

is an inner life which man may claim if he is blessed with awareness:

> Si no vuelven las horas vuelven las presencias
> En esta vida hay otra vida . . .
>
> (*Sal.* 44)

One step further and the presence becomes an intimation of the
divine, sometimes with an almost biblical flavour as in 'Amistad':

> No hay nadie
> La presencia sin nombre me rodea
>
> (*Sal.* 34)

Or again in 'Lauda' (*Sal.* 54–6), where the presence is felt, not
seen, and the vision is 'sin visiones entrevista'. 'Piedra de sol',
like other poems in *La estación violenta*, marks the point at which
Paz gives most open expression to his visions of transcendent
unity, and it is here that the presence becomes unmistakably a
'feeling of the numinous':[13]

> el mundo se despoja de sus máscaras
> y en su centro, vibrante transparencia,
> lo que llamamos Dios . . .
> plenitud de presencias y de nombres.
>
> (*Lib.* 249)

This is not a call to a personal comforter, but rather an archetypal
urge of man to experience the eternal, which is denied only with
danger.[14] The final appeal of 'Pidra de sol' is to a universal being
in which all consciousness can come to rest:

> rostro de mar, de pan, de roca y fuente,
> manantial que disuelve nuestros rostros
> en el rostro sin nombre, el ser sin rostro,
> indecible presencia de presencias . . .
>
> (*Lib.* 254)

'Sunyata', from *Ladera Este*, though imbued with a different
philosophy and written in a style which involves a much more
immediate synthesis of opposites, cannot avoid the use of the
same word in its approach to the same concept. The tree, which is
the objective correlative for the day, and that for existence,
becomes absorbed in a moment of ineffable glory:

Torbellino ágata
Presencia que se consume
En una gloria sin substancia . . .
(*L.E.* 97)

The establishment of a semiotic mode in Paz's poetry has not been done with any desire to broach a discussion of the poet's religious beliefs. It is certain that he sees himself fitting no ideological pigeon-hole, and in any case this issue is beside the point. It is the experience which the poems communicate which I have wished to examine, here from the point of view of the poet's language. The personal vocabulary of which any reader soon becomes aware is important, first because it provides the unifying motifs which bind together the total structure of the poet's work. Secondly the changes in meaning which these frequently used words embody are signposts along the trajectory which the poetry marks out for itself. While the tensions within the semiotic mode are primarily of a linguistic kind and the elements of which it is composed differ from the modes previously discussed, I believe that the paradigm which these elements trace out is identical with that of the mythic and the surrealist modes. That is to say that the structure underlying Paz's *œuvre* remains the same, no matter how it is approached: experience for Paz, both personal and linguistic, arranges itself in a cycle in which the threshold of consciousness expands after coming to grips with some sort of an initiatory rite, be it one of personal suffering or of creative turmoil. Language, in order to communicate this experience, establishes a poetic world in which intensity is expressed via qualities of light and time which become connected in the reader's mind with nuances of spiritual states. The reader is involved in the poet's experience through elements of Nature, through his own sensory perceptions (especially the visual), and through calls from the collective unconscious which find their echoes in everyone. This discussion of the semiotic mode has been an attempt to describe the shades of meaning implicit in the language upon which this poetic world rests.

IV

MODES IN HARMONY: PASSION
AND PARADOX

IT is by now apparent that whatever changes occur in the outer covering of Paz's poetry, the inner core is constant. At the heart of his poetic creation is the urge for what Lévy-Bruhl has called the 'participation mystique',[1] which is that metaphysical awareness of 'otherness', goal of all seekers after the transcendent. Though the means change, the end does not. The instinct which drives the creative artist to his medium is his vision of the primordial condition of things, a condition brought into tension by the striving of opposites to find harmony in union. Behind the mythic cycle of life, death, and rebirth, behind the surrealist exploring of the subconscious mind, as behind Paz's system of what might be called passwords, there lies the same search for the reconciling of opposites. Energy, in this case creative energy— the poem—comes from the inner polarity between contrary forces which demand an equilibrating process. This law of the human psyche was recognized long ago by Herodotus, and christened '*enantiodromia*, a running contrariwise, by which he meant that sooner or later everything runs into its opposite'.[2] It is the regulative factor in creative art as in the great religious systems, and as it is, indeed, in all manifestations of human life.[3]

There are two direct paths of the union of opposites with which this chapter will be concerned. One is emotive, one linguistic, but they are the purest expressions in human terms of this archetypal impulse. One is the meeting of male and female in erotic love, and the other the use of paradox as the nearest human approximation to that which is ineffable. That these cannot be separated will become clear in the discussion of 'Blanco', or indeed the later poems in *Ladera Este*, where the experience of sexual passion depends upon paradox for its communication. Passion has been a recurring state in Paz's life, so that poems in which the male and female principles harmonize in love are found from the early days onwards. Paradox in the later works performs the same function

that surrealism did earlier, though in a less opaque way. Both give
the poet a channel through which to explore the seemingly contradictory but actually complementary processes upon which the
life-force depends. But the succinctness and ambiguity of paradox
better suit a mature mind which sees at once to the heart of things.
To quote Jung: 'Unequivocal statements can be made only in
regard to immanent objects; transcendental ones can be expressed
only by paradox.'4

The use of paradox in the expression of passion is a later
characteristic of Paz's poetry, and is concurrent with his explorations
of Eastern mysticism. But there is another quality of his love-
poetry present in early as in late work, namely chthonic imagery.
Woman, that is the spirit of womanhood, like the *anima* within
the male psyche, is intuited as a mysterious and different kind of
being. She fascinates and yet is a source of awe; man is drawn to
her, yet resists. The power of love drives together two opposite
poles which are held apart by an equally strong resistance. Man
is aware of the incompleteness of his own nature which seeks out
the dangerous otherness of its opposite principle. Both the incompleteness and the yearning are the same feelings which turn man
towards the world of Nature, producing an animistic outlook in
primitive peoples who regard as reciprocal this tug between
themselves and the chain of being of which they are a part. All
the manifestations of the Great Mother Goddess bear witness to
this most basic instinct of man to incorporate himself in those
elements from which he stands separated. Thus when the poet
draws upon his psychic disposition, shaped by age-old forces of
heredity, it is in imagery from the natural world that he describes
that other principle with which he seeks reunion. Nature provides
the rhythms, the oppositions, the cycles, and the harmonies which
the love of man and woman reproduces in microcosm in each
love-affair and in each orgasm.

The great climax to Paz's poetry of passion is 'Blanco',
where chthonic imagery and paradox together communicate the
force of this experience which surges like a deep presentiment
of something primordial and irresistible. 'Blanco' is also the supreme
union of inspiration and medium. Yet the same experience,
the same in kind if not in degree, drives the poet in his twenty-
first year to write the love poems of *Primer día* (*Lib.* 13–17) and
Bajo tu clara sombra (*Lib.* 18–23).

'Soneto III' of *Primer día* (*Lib.* 15), with all its literary and biblical echoes, is a young man's tribute to the body of his loved one. The conceits are mannered and the images do not surprise by their originality ('Dos barcos de velamen desplegado / tus dos pechos . . .'). What one remembers of the poem is rather the emphasis on the colour green and the juxtaposition of opposing concepts: 'quema y vuelve yelo', 'sol y bruma'. The association of chthonic green with physical love is a commonplace in poetry,[5] and green here connects the vegetative realm with the feelings emanating from the poet's sexual desires. Thus the girl's hair has taken 'verdecido júbilo' from the sky, the wind among the leaves blows a green rain upon her back, and her body yields to love 'bajo el verde cielo adolescente'. The colour green emphasizes the symbolism which will run through all three volumes of Paz's work, allowing woman and manifestations of erotic love to be lyricized in every possible sort of nature image. The juxtaposition of contrasting elements as in the description of the girl's neck ('Es otoño en tu nuca: sol y bruma') is an early example of that dialectical approach of the mind which must syphon into poetry psychic events which are themselves ambivalent. Imagination draws upon the ambiguity of mind and of life itself, and the attempt to harmonize this vital polyvalency is seen as clearly in this early example as in Paz's surrealist poems, or in the paradoxes of his last works.

'Bajo tu clara sombra' (*Lib.* 18–23) is a love poem with three characters—the poet, the beloved, and Nature—these last two fused to such an extent that they are at times indistinguishable. The poem rises to a climax in which the union of man and woman is duplicated by the union of themselves with Nature. Obviously the inspiration for chthonic imagery lies, at this point in the poet's life, in a monist metaphysic. The dialectic of love inspires the opening lines:

> Bajo tu clara sombra
> vivo como la llama al aire,
> en tenso aprendizaje de lucero.
> > (*Lib.* 18)

It is this same dialectic within a wider frame which brings the poem full circle at its close, when man and woman, now united, assume their living (therefore resistive) place in the great design:

canto, cantamos
bajo tus anchas manos que nos llueven,
como dos hierbas puras,
como un árbol azul,
tal una sola flor que te resiste.

(*Lib.* 23)

To reach this state of resolved tension the poet moves between two points, at once separate and indistinguishable, the power of the feminine and the power of Nature, fused at one time in the loved woman's body, at another in the beauty of the physical universe. Woman embodies the life-force, her footprint is the 'centro visible de la tierra', her voice brings back the spark of energy without which the universe dies:

nos anuncia el rescate de las aguas,
el regreso del fuego,
la vuelta de la espiga . . .

(*Lib.* 18)

She is Prometheus, Ceres, the arcane substance of the alchemists ('un metal escondido'), and the pulse of her blood is that of 'las mareas / que alzan las orillas del planeta'.

The life-force surrounds them, in the dust and in the water, and in the 'callado círculo' of the ash-trees with its hint of magic. They recognize it in each other's bodies, the male instinct like the 'brusca sacudida / con que desnuda el aire los jardines', hers still and deep as water, 'mar profundo que duerme entre dos mares'. In 'Piedra de sol', more than twenty years later, Paz will see a world being born when two people kiss. The same thought is present now:

Mira el poder del mundo:
reconócete ya, al reconocerme.

(*Lib.* 20)

Thus two bodies become one and the poem soars into a realm of light, like a river 'que navega perdido / sin asir una orilla'. It is the calm at the centre of the vortex—'hasta los quietos cielos / donde vibra el instante'—where all promise of fruition comes to pass: 'la plenitud del mundo y de sus formas'.

Then the poet expands his horizon, so that the force of Nature felt through the woman is also recognized as a greater whole in which all has its place. To this matrix all may be entrusted, for every vital urge is sanctified by it:

> mi cuerpo, que me fija
> y en sus huesos limita mi destino,
> y el cuerpo que se abre
> y en su tímida gracia me sostiene.
>
> (*Lib.* 22)

The awareness of his own vitality and his love for his woman are both manifestations of the life-force from which they are drawn and to which they may safely be recommitted. The circle is completed. The shadow and the flame of the opening are one in an all-embracing concord.

The variations upon this theme are endless, and *Libertad bajo palabra* presents an *embarras de richesse*. The same strains appear and reappear: the male seeks completeness in woman, and the urge for this completeness is the basic source of energy in life as in Paz's poetic creation. Woman herself is a polarity of forces which attract and which terrify, expressed in imagery linking these forces to those of Nature, and the transcendence which is achieved in the moment of passion is recognized in terms of the great chain of being experienced to the full. Thus the rite of passage to a higher awareness is consistently found by Paz in erotic love, expressed in these earlier works with an extraversion and an exuberance which his later, more mature spirituality alters in degree but not in kind.

Though examples of chthonic imagery and of the harmony of opposites in passion abound in *Libertad bajo palabra*, their essence is uniform, and the poems quoted may suffice as examples. *Salamandra* presents a similar concept in more opaque fashion, and the equation of woman with Nature, likewise of sexual with cosmic harmony, is transmitted through oblique and complex expression. 'Paisaje pasional' (*Sal.* 66–7) may be interpreted as the sensation of passion objectified in Nature, but in Nature transfigured by the heat of an imagination reaching into the subconscious for connections and comparisons. Only in the penultimate line is the presence of the loved one specified, and then it is the centre of her soul which is mentioned. The poem has worked from the physical exterior through the moment of ecstasy to the inner experience without one break in the gigantic metaphor in whose terms the body is the 'paisaje pasional' where all elements blend.

The poem opens with a paradoxical image, stone fruit, which then becomes the fruit of time. The years resist all but the inexorable glance of love—they are 'años negros carmesíes morados', they are empty space, they are 'Granito basalto corales desgarrados'. Images are designed to express the pain and the inevitability of ecstasy: space is 'hendido' by love; the fruit is 'abierto por una mirada . . . inexorable'; the brow of fire is rent by 'cicatrices de sal'. This metaphor is especially powerful in that salt for the alchemists represented both the bitterness and the wisdom of Eros, which the feeling power of woman could bestow.[6] Thus salt and fire together create an associative field, which, added to all the connotations of forbidden fruit and the mention of pomegranate so significant in the Demeter and Persephone myth, has established in seven lines ever-widening circles of erotic and emotional content without any direct allusions to the presumed occasion of the poem.

The surrealist description of the setting continues, coloured now by expressions which build up a threatening atmosphere. A star shines over 'desfiladeros', presumably of love, but it is an 'astro iracundo', and the valleys below are 'valles de jade y sangre', shining, precious, but associated with pain. The snow and the moon (both symbols of chastity) converse 'a la intemperie' and a multiplication of moons shines down on 'bosques abolidos'. The opposition heightens between resistive matter and irresistible force. The day is 'petrificado', but the emptiness of space is torn open by the beak of the 'ave solar'. Earth-bound Nature is heavy with metaphors of precious stones and of time ('los pechos inmensos de ámbar y el ágata . . . el río y su manto de edades'), but it is not immune from the effect of the stars:

> Sobre el abismo desnudo como el primer grito
> Huellas rojas pisadas de astros . . .
>
> (*Sal.* 66)

Fire can overcome everything as the vine can cover the rock. The tension increases as the conflict of energies is concentrated in the same image, instead of in two in juxtaposition. Now the landscape is like a sleeping lion, or a feast of flames. Elements go contrary to their natural impulse—'Materias extasiadas ríos parados'.

Movement and stillness are joined in single images as manifestations of the energy emanating from opposites in conflict—'Extensiones espacios reinos del ala desplegada / Tempestad fija'. The magic moment of insight comes at the heart of the vortex, 'Instante suspendido en el centro vibrante / Entre quietud y movimiento', and the poet feels the vibrations of being on some vast and cosmic plane as the hurricane advances, its eyes 'cerrados . . . hinchados de visiones', in a perfect transference of the subjective emotion to the perceived object (the experience of self attributed to the 'otherness' which is its cause). Then the hurricane passes through the outer selves of the lovers to 'el centro de tu alma', and the poem ends with a line which links the cycle of love, individual or collective, erotic or sentimental, to the great cycle of life itself, given, experienced, and transmitted: 'Lo que aplasta su pie derecho reverdece bajo el izquierdo' (*Sal.* 67).

Another poem set entirely in chthonic imagery is 'Temporal' (*Sal.* 80–1). Here there is no fulfilment of erotic passion, but the tension of the intricate emotional reactions between the sexes is simulated in the imagistic tensions of the poem. The woman's body is asleep, watched or evoked by the poet, and counterbalanced by a torrent on a mountain at night. The poem moves between the two scenes, the sleeping woman and the raging stream, juxtaposing and superimposing images to build up the feeling of dynamism. Thus the stream is at once an objective correlative for the primeval power inherent in the woman's body and so deeply felt by the poet, and also for the turbulence which this body, itself passive in sleep, creates in the mind of the beholder.

The poem opens with darkness and the sound of the water ('el torrente delira en voz alta'), both of which create an atmosphere of instinctive, hidden passion. Water particularly evokes images of fertility, of life, and of sexual fluids, made all the more powerful by the personification of the verb 'delira'. The reader at once senses by extension a human being crying aloud in troubled sleep, an impression strengthened by the immediate appearance of the sleeping woman who moves forward 'entre precipicios' and whose sleeping body is troubled by the wind (again symbolic of the *pneuma*, the breath of life, here the life-force inherent in sex): 'El viento lucha a oscuras con tu sueño.' The double image continues with the foliage on the mountain and the tossing body— 'maraña verde y blanca'—the colour green linking the vegetative world with that of eroticism and procreation. After the confusion of tangled undergrowth the long *i*'s of the next line and the unexpected assonance produce a beautiful *rallentando* which keeps alive the peacefulness of sleep alongside the frenetic energy of the mountain stream: 'Encina niña encina milenaria'. The wind then becomes the dominant motif and the girl's mind is tossed and buffeted, dragged and thrown—'abre tu pensamiento y lo dispersa.' Her relaxed body is caught up in her psychic whirlwind:

> Torbellino tus ojos
> Torbellino tu ombligo . . .
> *(Sal.* 80)

The wind storms around and through her:

> Temporal en tu frente
> Temporal en tu nuca y en tu vientre . . .
> *(Sal.* 80)

And the wind finally brings together the woman-image and the stream-image which are then fused for the rest of the poem:

> Como una rama seca te avienta
> El viento
> A lomos del torrente de tu sueño . . .
> *(Sal.* 80)

Now the interpretation of imagery and symbolism is complete. Mountain stream and woman together—'Manos verdes y pies negros'—her body is now 'de montaña dormida', the stream flows between her thighs with the same delirium of pebbles and water; her forehead is a cliff where a river of birds passes, birds so often associated by Paz with desire felt or fulfilled. The mountain woods are personified and somehow subjugated to the wind of life within her, and the raging of the stream rises higher while her body sinks deeper into sleep in an ever darker night:

> Cada vez más alto
> El torrente delira
> Cada vez más hondo
> Por tu cuerpo dormido
> Cada vez más noche
> *(Sal.* 81)

The tension is not resolved but heightened in this climax where the polarity between opposites is made extreme—noise and silence, sleep and life-force—to end in all the energy of unsatisfied passion. The delving into the sleeping mind, here not the poet's but his woman's, brings us close to the Surrealists' deliberate penetration of hidden regions of the psyche. Likewise Paz has gone behind outer reality to explore inner realms and has set one in opposition to the other, the antithesis never being brought to synthesis but allowed to end in tense expectancy. For the expression of these opposing tendencies he has turned to the natural world and picked in contrast to the relaxed passivity of a sleeping body the turbulence of a mountain stream and a stormy wind at night. The erotic power of these images in an oblivious body communicates perfectly the antagonism between male and female principles and between the subconscious world of the unbridled imagination and the controlled world of the conscious mind. While the sexual urge is left in unsatisfied tension, the brilliant fusing of the two images does present an aesthetic synthesis of opposing forces. The poem itself, typically in Paz's work, is the point of union of the two poles of the creative mind, one imaginative, the other rational, or in other words the one drawing upon primordial impulses and the other filtered through the process of personal experience.

There is a poem in *Ladera Este* which translates into poetic terms the process just described above. It is 'Perpetua encarnada' (*L.E.* 36–9), and in his note (*L.E.* 175) Paz says that he is using this 'planta herbácea anual cuyas flores persisten meses enteros sin padecer alteración' as an objective correlative for poetry: 'En el poema: la poesía, el lenguaje'. The equating of poetry with language is interesting in itself, for it explicitly brings to light a process which has already been commented on in earlier chapters of this study.

The opening of the poem is again a setting in Nature, here a hot, dazzling day with its contrasts of light and shade and in its centre the sun, pulsating with a life so vivid that it is immobile: 'un amarillo remolino / Una sola intensidad monótona . . .' The scene is developed in this contrast between the luxuriant earth with its 'verde algarabía', its palpitating animal life, and its play of light and dark, while over all hangs the illusion of a motionless sun: 'Gloria inmóvil que un parpadeo / Vuelve añicos . . .' Time hangs in a Wordsworthian expectancy as the poet watches a tiny lizard moving with the same potential life-force that he feels in himself and all around him. This life-force is the chain of being, the manifestation of self or of mind, in Buddhist terms, with which he can identify as sentient being:

> Mareo
> Pululación y vacío
> La tarde la bestezuela mi conciencia
> Una vibración idéntica indiferente . . .
> (*L.E.* 37)

In the shade of the eucalyptus trees he begs for sameness in Nature ('Pedí a su sombra / Llueva o truene / Ser siempre igual'), just as he desires wholeness within himself ('Pedí templanza pedí perseverancia'). The world is too much with him ('Prendido prendado / Estoy enamorado de este mundo'), and he needs detachment so that he may open his eyes and see the connections, the interlocking harmonies at whose heart lies poetry, his absolute in human terms:

> Pido entereza pido desprendimiento
> Abrir los ojos
> Evidencias ilesas
> Entre las claridades que se anulan
> No la abolición de las imágenes
> La encarnación de los pronombres
> El mundo que entre todos inventamos
> Pueblo de signos
> Y en su centro
> La solitaria
> *Perpetua encarnada* . . .
> (*L.E.* 38)

If the world we know is conceptualized and perceived only through language, then poetry is the point beyond dialectic, and only paradox can express the 'otherness' of its essence. 'Thus it is and is not, that is to say, not to be found in our experience.'[7] In this case poetry, language, is

> Una mitad mujer
> Peña manantial la otra
> Palabra de todos con que hablamos a solas . . .
> (*L.E.* 38)

As the nexus of irreconcilables reconciled, it is for Paz 'Razón del hombre', and the insight he has received spreads outwards from

himself to illuminate the time and place in which the experience
and the poem both began:

> La noche se congrega y se ensancha
> Nudo de tiempos y racimo de espacios
> Veo oigo respiro
> Pido ser obediente a este día y esta noche
>
> (*L.E.* 39)

As is often the case, the poet comes to the moment of vision in the
loneliness of the night when distractions and contraries of the
day-time are obscured. Thus the line of paradox is pursued:
enlightenment is accompanied by outer darkness, and the feeling
of communion with an absolute arrives in moments of solitude.

Ladera Este contains other varieties of paradox with other
resolutions. A similar pattern links the short poem 'Himachal
Pradesh (3)' (*L.E.* 70–1) with the magnificent 'Viento entero'
(101–8). Both face the problem of political protest in an apathetic
world, and in both cases Paz achieves his effect by allowing the
element of violence to break the previously established mood of
the poem. There are three short poems written in Himachal
Pradesh, which Paz's note (*L.E.* 178) tells us is a state in the
Western Himalayas, where the Vedic hymns were possibly composed. They are interspersed with three 'Intermitencias del
Oeste' so that the six short poems together interweave the immediate experience of the poet in India and his awareness of and
reactions to events in the outside world. The third Himachal
Pradesh poem carries this formal juxtaposition into its own content
like an effect of interior duplication. It opens with ambiguous
references to evil, first the '5 pequeñas abominaciones / vistas,
oídas, cometidas', and then the scene of the vultures and the
lame eagle awaiting 'su resto de carroña'. Interpretations spring
to mind, but Paz offers none; the carrion birds merely provide the
background for the strangeness of the human scenes he describes:
the barrister in his dak bungalow, the 'pareja de viejitos' quarrel-
ling, the anachronistic English commenting on the cricket-match.
These scenes than fall into relief as the poet's consciousness expands
to fill the forefront of the poem and of the reader's attention:

> un astro negro se abre en mi frente
> como una granada (EN PARÍS PRENDEN FUEGO
> A LA BOLSA, TEMPLO DEL CAPITALISMO . . .
>
> (*L.E.* 71)

Human endeavours and antagonisms flash with ironic futility across the quiet scene as across the helpless awareness of the poet:

> Polvo y gritos de pájaros
> sobre la tarde quemada.
> Yo escribo estas líneas infames.
> (*L.E.* 71)

'Infames' perhaps because of the actual futility of the metaphysical in the world of physical existence.

'Viento entero' (*L.E.* 101–8) is one of Paz's major poems of recent years. It is rich in associations and allusions which set up a chain of connections in the reader's mind producing a complexity which defies explication. Yet at its base it relies on the paradox of a world in which love can exist alongside hate and aggression. Its enigma is that of man himself, capable at once of spiritual greatness and animal brutality. It is a love poem, then, whose lyric tone is shattered by scenes of human cruelty which flash into the poet's mind even at moments of the most tender union with his beloved. This union is conceived of as the gateway out of daily chronology into the timelessness of myth. 'Viento entero' opens the collection of poems called 'Hacia el comienzo', and it sets in contrast to each other the time of history, with its events, places, and people, and the circular time into which love introduces us and where we find the suspended moment and the roots of our spiritual being. The first line establishes the paradox upon which the moment of love depends—'El presente es perpetuo.' The mountains stand as symbols of a fixed principle in human affairs, 'Están aquí desde el principio', but the wind, associated with the *pneuma* of love and of life, has just been born: 'El viento acaba de nacer / Sin edad / Como la luz y como el polvo.' The poem moves from this initial dialectic through a series of scenes connecting the mythic world of love with the actual moments of a love odyssey. The first description is of an Indian bazaar, which the poet presumably contemplates while memory begins to stir within him. It also is seen in terms of contrasts: the shouts of the children cut across 'los claros de silencio', and the beggars by the river are 'príncipes en harapos'.

The vividness of this day ('El día salta / Ágata / El pájaro caído') is the transition to a day in Paris when the unreality of meaningless acts of daily life was disrupted by the vividness of a girl, 'Una muchacha real / Entre las casas y las gentes espectrales'. In herself she combines the age-old symbolic opposites of fire and water which reappear time and again in alchemy, religion, and magic:

> Si el agua es fuego
> Llama
> En el centro de la hora redonda . . .
> (*L.E.* 102)

This paradox reappears as a motif accompanying the appearance of the beloved throughout this and other love poems of 'Hacia el comienzo' to its final climax in 'Blanco'. The union of fire and water is connected both traditionally and in Paz's poetry with a transcendence of the world of differentiation and the achieving of a higher truth. In 'Viento entero' it marks the 'eternal return' which is the mythic finding of lost origins:

> Juntos atravesamos
> Los cuatro espacios los tres tiempos
> Pueblos errantes de reflejos
> Y volvimos al día del comienzo . . .
> (*L.E.* 102)

With no break in its flow the poem returns to the present moment of composition, the summer solstice, symbolically the zenith of the natural cycle. Now the loved woman's presence is recognized. She is reading, lying naked on a red quilt, but the poet's contemplation of her body and their mutual joy are interrupted by the other awareness which he cannot banish from consciousness, that of human brutality, which runs like a linking motif through history. Oppression in Santo Domingo in 1965, defeat of Mexico by the U.S. in 1847, Muslim cruelty in the eighteenth century are all manifestations of the age-old human impulse to cruelty, though a possibly optimistic note is sounded:

> Las manos abrasadas
> Los constructores de catedrales y pirámides
> Levantarán sus casas transparentes . . .
> (*L.E.* 103)

This is the moment of greatest polarity in the poem. It now becomes a slow fusion of male and female against a changing background of scenes: the palace-castle of Datia, the mountain pass of Garganta of Salang, the Usbek region, Bactriana; then

Mount Kalaisa where the embrace of man and woman recapitu-
lates the divine love of Shiva and Parvati, and Lahor in the final
moment when the threads are gathered together. The poem comes
full circle thematically as motifs combine—fire and water, male
and female in the renewed cycle:

> Yo veo a través de mis actos irreales
> El mismo día que comienza . . .
>
> (*L.E.* 108)

In the poems which enter the realm of metaphysics proper the use
of paradox recalls that of the mystics, especially Santa Teresa and
San Juan. Obviously the ineffable can be expressed only in terms
of what it is not, since by definition it exceeds our experiential
realm. Earlier descriptions of 'Sunyata' and 'Lectura de John
Cage' have approached this problem in the context of the mythic
mode whose most sublime expression is reached in paradoxical
language, especially that of Mahayana Buddhism. The precept
'Samsara es Nirvana' synthesizes the most lofty concept of the
doctrine of the Great Ferry-boat. One recalls the Zen koans as
well as oxymorons of the 'Vivo sin vivir en mí' pattern of Santa
Teresa. The poet who struggles with the most recondite experiences
of the psyche will turn to the age-old imagery of mythology or to
the contradictions of paradox in order to express the inexpressible
weirdness of his vision. At the line which divides the visionary
from the psychological artist, in Jung's terminology, synthesis is
achieved only through the dialectic of apparently contradictory
portions of what an enlightened vision sees as a wider whole.

'BLANCO'

'Blanco' (1966) is Octavio Paz's most recent masterpiece, and
its complexities are overwhelming. The starting-point for this
attempted explication of the poem is a quotation from Paz himself, which appears in his introductory note to the catalogue for the
Tantric Art exhibition in Paris during the spring of 1970. Having
discussed the obvious thirst in our day for art as a ritual of crea-
tivity, as the 'incarnation des images qui pourrait satisfaire cette
nécessité de rites collectifs qu'éprouve notre monde', Paz specu-
lates upon our need not to neglect the other direction in which art
can lead us, namely, towards meditation and solitary contemplation.
Art of this kind would result neither in the idolatry of the 'chose

artistique' nor in the Dadaesque destruction of the object, but would see the painting, sculpture, or poem as a point of departure. 'Vers où? Vers la présence, vers l'absence, vers l'ailleurs . . . Non pas la restauration de l'objet d'art mais l'instauration du poème ou du tableau comme un signe inaugural qui ouvre le chemin.'[8] 'Blanco' appears to be an example of such a poem, and its ultimate importance lies in its combination of the realms of art and of metaphysics; that is, it expresses a transcendence which is aesthetic and erotic, but which by association and image reaches to other levels of experience. The title itself would be an immediate case in point, calling to mind at once the blankness of *sunyata*, the void or absolute of Mahayana Buddhism, and the combination of all colours of the spectrum in white light. Significantly, the title for Paz's essay in the Tantric Art catalogue is 'La Pensée en blanc' which sets up a similar associative field of meaning.

Nor is 'Blanco' a poem explicable merely by textual exegesis, for it draws upon the thematicism of music and upon the visual effects of graphic art as well. What is as important as the poem itself is the space which surrounds it, which its presence displaces physically and its reading temporally, and which then closes over it once it is read and put away. But it will have acted as a sign, taking us as the poet says 'de lo "en blanco" a lo blanco — al blanco',[9] and elsewhere Paz points out the forgotten metaphor which still leads us in Spanish from 'signo' back to the Latin 'signum', also the root of 'sino', destiny.[10] Thus the double meaning behind Paz's note to 'Blanco' as it appears in *Ladera Este* (p. 145): 'debería leerse como una sucesión de signos sobre una página única.' In the original, boxed edition the reader brings the poem into being, physically as well as intellectually, by unfolding the paper on which it is printed, as by responding to its content. Thus the reading in time corresponds to the space physically displaced by the progressively growing object which is the text. Space becomes a metaphor for time, a visible measuring-tape, as it were, and as the work appears the typography maps out the different parts of the text by variations of typeface and contrasting red and black columns, until there results a sort of typographic mandala whose constituent portions represent its regions, colours, symbols, and figures. Like the mandala, like the act of sexual union, the poem acts as a bridge to the beyond, to the target —'al blanco'—which it remains to each of us to define for himself.

Since the reading of poetry is necessarily a linear and temporal act, the parts of this poetic mandala must be combined by the volition of the reader, and the poet gives a variety of suggestions. Briefly, the poem consists of a central column which opens and closes in a light-face type with widely spaced lettering, consolidating into bold-face type for most of its length. This centrally descending text is interrupted at four points by a double column, black on the left and red on the right. The left-hand column represents an erotic poem divided into four moments which correspond to the four traditional elements; the right-hand column constitutes a poem complete in itself and exploring in turn sensation, perception, imagination, and understanding. The central column is the linguistic adventure from silence through expression to silence again, passing, according to the poet, 'por cuatro estados: amarillo, rojo, verde y azul', colours especially significant in Tantric representations. These individual poems may be combined in several ways. Thus in the intention of the poem, in its graphic form, and in the colours which it invokes, 'Blanco' is close to the world of the *Hevajra Tantra*, a quotation from which opens the poem: 'By passion the world is bound, by passion too it is released.'

Since in book form the parallel with the 'rollo de pinturas y emblemas tántricos' (*L.E.* 145) is necessarily lost, the typographical variations must assume more importance: the left-hand (black) column begins with a regular margin, and the right-hand (red) column is sometimes set off and capitalized so as to be separate from the other, sometimes merely runs on from it line by line. In either case the left-hand is set in heavier type and the right-hand in red italics. The three columns do not appear at the same time: in hopscotch form the central block is followed by the two side by side, and the pattern is repeated three times, ending with a single block. Thus starting on 'tierra' we can reach 'cielo' in eight jumps, but we have not progressed in a straight line; we have rather curved back on ourselves in thematic recapitulation.

In the Joaquín Mortiz edition of *Ladera Este* (1969), 'Blanco' is printed sideways on the page, and with the need to flick over pages visual effects require more intellectual attention than should be the case, since one's experience is thereby diluted by reflection. Division of sections is indicated by capitalization—the opening is in lower case, the second section much capitalized, the third not, and so on. There are six central sections ('tierra' has an ante-chamber, i.e. the opening thirteen lines), as opposed to the four left-hand and four right-hand. Paz suggests the following six permutations for the reader:

(a) En su totalidad, como un solo texto;

(b) la columna del centro, con exclusión de las de izquierda y derecha, es un poema cuyo tema es el tránsito de la palabra, del silencio al silencio (de lo 'en blanco' a lo blanco — al blanco), pasando por cuatro estados: amarillo, rojo, verde y azul;

(c) la columna de la izquierda es un poema erótico dividido en cuatro momentos que corresponden a los cuatro elementos tradicionales;

(d) la columna de la derecha es otro poema, contrapunto del anterior y compuesto de cuatro variaciones sobre la sensación, la percepción, la imaginación y el entendimiento;

(e) cada una de las cuatro partes formadas por dos columnas puede leerse, sin tener en cuenta esa división, como un solo texto: cuatro poemas independientes;

(f) la columna del centro puede leerse como seis poemas sueltos y las de izquierda y derecha como ocho. (L.E. 145)

Musical terms most easily describe the poem's thematic pro-gression. The double portions contain the leitmotiv which is at the heart of Paz's poetic vision: sexual union gives man direct knowledge of a cosmic unity in the light of which alone existence has meaning. In a form itself an objective correlative of this theme, the poet struggles alone with his thoughts and words in the single blocks, breaking through to the synthetic vision in the double sections where through woman he achieves experiential security. Interrupting theme, development, and counter-theme, the melody of the leitmotiv sings out four times, until in the final single section all paradox merges in the epistemological truth which the leitmotiv has been insistently suggesting:

> El mundo
> Haz de tus imágenes
> Anegadas en la música
> Tu cuerpo
> Derramado en mi cuerpo
> Visto
> Desvanecido
> Da realidad a la mirada
> (L.E. 169)

At the core of Paz's poetic vision lies the desire for this epistemological security. From his early years his work is a search for
ways by which man may become aware of and hold to his metaphysical identity. 'Blanco' is one of the purest examples of this
search. The poet has language, man has his senses, his intuition,
and his power to love, and with these alone Paz tries in 'Blanco'
to explore the nature of reality, of poetry, and of knowledge. The
engagement of the reader's senses of touch, sight, and hearing is
legitimate in that Paz tries to show the comprehensive nature of
this exploration.

'In the beginning was the Word . . .', the word which binds,
from which all else grows:

> el comienzo
>   el cimiento
> la simiente
>   latente
>   (*L.E.* 147)

The unusual (for Paz) consonance and assonance of the opening
four words carry to the unconscious mind through the ear an
intuition of the concept which the conscious mind will grasp
analytically. The rhyme and the meaning of 'latente' subtly
reinforce the hidden power of the seed, as of the word, ready at
some time to grow and give fruit. Thus 'Blanco' opens with
seemingly biblical certainty, but at once moves to paradox in
which lies the human enigma—words, so full of potential, yet so
fallible:

> inaudita   inaudible
>   impar
> grávida   nula
>   (*L.E.* 147)

Then an image which expresses the constant horror and frustration
of the poet:

> la enterrada con los ojos abiertos
> inocente   promiscua
>   la palabra
> sin nombre   sin habla
>   (*L.E.* 147)

Yet the poet must work with the inadequacy of words, in the
constant tension of language,

> Bajo la piel de la penumbra
> Late una lámpara.
>
> (*L.E.* 148)

The lamp shines through 'las confusiones taciturnas', stubbornly protecting 'caídas realidades', as a sunflower stays upright, though it may be asleep or dead, and the gold of its blossom rusted. And in an imaginary hand, like a flower not seen or thought, only heard, the word appears:

> Amarillo
> Cáliz de consonantes y vocales
> Incendiadas . . .
>
> (*L.E.* 149)

Fire is the first transition motif, as the double block now takes up and develops the image:

> en el muro la sombra del fuego   *llama rodeada de leones* . . .
>
> (*L.E.* 150)

The girl laughs in a garden of flame, and their passion is that 'de la brasa compasiva'.

Word and poet are again alone in the next single block, which the water motif opens ('Oleaje de sílabas húmedas') and closes ('Hasta la ondulación, / El cabrilleo, / Hasta el agua'). Fire and water combine in the mystic symbol of the Nahuas as the poet fights through language to establish some identity for himself as Mexican and as man. He feels 'un presentimiento de lenguaje' pulsing within him and he waits for the words to form as Livingstone for the river to rise. The river image takes over as a symbol of the poet's life or way 'rojo . . . entre sableras llameantes', passing between arid signs of fortuitous destruction ('naipes rotos'). The fire–water myth, already noted as typical of Paz's vision of dynamic harmony, is an ironic hieroglyph 'En el pecho de México caído'. Yet this is his heritage and his starting-place ('Polvo soy de aquellos lodos'), and by his self-acknowledgement he is freed to an awareness of the universal irony of the human condition:

> Boca de manantial
> Amordazado
> Por la conjuración anónima
> De los huesos . . .
>
> (*L.E.* 152)

The harshness of the image of the gagged stream of language moves jerkily, roughly, through ideas of expiation, imprisonment, and murder to 'El muerto innumerable', who cannot find any release in words at all. Sense is expressed in sound, uncompromising and difficult to the tongue ('propiciación', 'emparedado'). To speak while others work 'Es pulir huesos', a powerful and double-edged image, with its connotations of death, dehumanization, and the callousness of a craftsman who works on what remains of a living being; yet at the same time an object of lasting beauty may emerge from what was merely a process of decay. The poet's words by contrast may 'sharpen silences' for us, give us a window ('la transparencia') to widen our vision. Now the verse becomes gentler with the sibilants of 'Aguzar / Silencios', which pick up the double evocation of 'huesos' and continue through the lines like the murmur of a stream, and into the second double section which becomes a rhapsody of love in water imagery.

The keyword of this transition is 'transparencia', which expresses one of Paz's central epistemological insights. Art, here 'pulir huesos', involves man in a struggle which he must undertake, with all the consequent suffering and frustration, to gain the few but infinitely precious moments of insight ('transparencia', 'presencia', 'instante') into the wholeness of created being. This is a mystic journey, followed by many in different ways, to which Paz feels himself committed as a man who has known the existential anguish of solitude, and who has transcended it in poetry and in love. The new awareness of reality brings new epistemological puzzles, but these can be resolved only in terms of this further dimension, that is, poetically and passionately, as the rest of 'Blanco' goes on to show.

The second double section is separated typographically on the page and there is no capitalization, a visual device which echoes the flowing-river motif. The right- and left-hand passages are complementary, the former more actual, the latter more abstract, but both centring on the act of sexual union as a confluence of rivers leading to a new realm of perception, both by the senses and by the intellect. The poet's self-awareness proves his own existence to him—in such a moment he cannot deny himself—and his own reality implies an echoing reality in that which surrounds him and which he perceives. The eye is seen as the dominant organ of sense perception, and it both reflects and returns his gaze, thus acknowledging his existence and making known its own:

> me miro en lo que miro
> como entrar por mis ojos
> en un ojo más límpido
> me mira lo que miro
> (*L.E.* 154)

By the act of perception we create the reality that surrounds us, since it gains recognition (and thus reality) only by our perceiving it:

> *es mi creación esto que veo*
> *la percepción es creación*
> (*L.E.* 154)

And the converse also holds true: 'I am myself and my circumstances', to quote Ortega y Gasset: '*soy la creación de lo que veo.*' Thus in the passionate acceptance and recognition one of the other, man and woman affirm their own reality and each other's in the momentary unity which bestows its own clairvoyance: 'La transparencia es todo lo que queda.'

The next single section expresses the poet's mood of desperation in an apocalyptic landscape of violent colours, shadows, and sounds. The poet seems isolated within a hostile, desert land of 'púas invisibles', 'buitres ahitos', an implacable sun, and colours which 'se obstinan'. The sky is black with crows, with 'violencias violetas', with sandstorms, with 'La cerrazón de reses de ceniza'. The order of Nature is disturbed ('Mugen los árboles encadenados'), and drums, flutes, thunder, and lightning fill the atmosphere as the poet seeks to fight his way out:

> Te golpeo cielo
>   Tierra te golpeo
> Cielo abierto tierra cerrada
> (*L.E.* 157)

(The analogy of the hopscotch again intrudes with a vision of man trapped between 'tierra' and 'cielo', threatened by both, not knowing which way to move.) But we are earth-bound by our nature; on earth it is given us to find even our heaven, as Tlaloc, god of rain, ruled over the Nahuas' Terrestrial Paradise.[11] So the earth bursts with the promise of new birth as Persephone returns, fertility and love survive, and the earth-word grows green. The poet finds his voice, which is his own intimation of immortality:

> Te abres tierra
> Tienes la boca llena de agua
> Tu cuerpo chòrrea cielo
> Tremor
> > Tu panza tiembla
> Tus semillas estallan
> > > Verdea la palabra
> > > (*L.E.* 157)

Motifs of earth and seed-time lead to the third double section, where the images which describe the love act are first of movement, as though echoing pursuit—'se desata se esparce / se levanta se erige Ídolo'—and then of the earth itself:

> inmóvil bajo el sol inmóvil *pradera quemada*
> del color de la tierra *color de sol en la arena*
> > (*L.E.* 158)

For the first time left- and right-hand columns run into each other, which produces an amazing speed and interpenetration of image and idea, as the eye is forced down and across the page at the same time. The woman's body becomes the focal point where intuition ('presencias') is grasped and where paradox is resolved:

> en la mujer desnuda *snap-shot de un latido de tiempo*
> pirausta nudo de presencias *real irreal quieto vibrante*
> > (*L.E.* 158)

Through the naked form of the woman the poet takes visible cognizance of the world which her life-force seems to personify:

> mujer tendida *hecha a la imagen del mundo*
> El mundo haz de tus imágenes
> > (*L.E.* 158)

The images of this section all convey a pulsating life which communicates at once the intuitive nature of the vision which the poet achieves and the quickening rhythm of the sex act itself: 'reverberación . . . girando girando . . . pensamiento gavilán . . . cabra en la peña hendida . . . snap-shot de un latido de tiempo . . . pirausta . . . vibrante . . . lluvia . . . pájaros.'

The poet has so far worked from single to double sections through transitions of fire, water, and earth imagery. The next single section leads through a dissolving illusory world in which his senses cease to guide him, to a point where space and thought both fade away around him and the transition occurs in the emptiness of space.

The atmosphere is one of disintegration, and of dizziness. The eye is bewildered by changing colours: the poet feels his control over language slipping away:

> La palabra se asoma a remolinos
> Azules.
>
> (*L.E.* 159)

The senses lose their ability to differentiate, or to grasp the reality of changing forms around a constant centre:

> Gira el anillo beodo,
> Giran los cinco sentidos
> Alrededor de la amatista
> Ensimismada.
>
> (*L.E.* 159)

In the resulting dazzlement the functions of thought, sight, hearing, and reason become mingled:

> Los reflejos, los pensamientos veo.
> Las precipitaciones de la música,
> El número cristalizado.
>
> (*L.E.* 160)

Hints of clarity and truth are annulled in the poet's metaphysical anguish, as he is confronted by 'La cara en blanco del olvido, / El resplandor de lo vacío'. He loses awareness of his own reality, for his shadow disappears, and his path takes him amid 'bosques impalpables . . . sinfines, Desfiladeros afilados'. His footsteps dissolve in space, which itself vanishes, and his mind in thoughts not of his creation.

In this existential vortex, through bewilderment and paradox the poet reaches a vision of undifferentiated being. The three paths along which he seeks the validity of his own experience, thought, language, and passion, combine in a gigantic assertion. Right-hand column again runs on from left-hand, and seems more closely linked, horizontally, i.e. the second portion amplifies or orchestrates the first, though the columns still have their original coherence.

The space motif carries through the opening eight lines, as the reality of the beloved also whirls in meaningless space, not affirming but questioning existence:

> caes de tu cuerpo a tu sombra
> en un caer inmóvil de cascada . . .
> (*L.E.* 162)

But past and present become one ('en un presente que no acaba'); beginning and end meet ('caes en tu comienzo') as male and female complete the union of opposites which is the archetypal resolution of the cosmic paradox:

> *el firmamento es macho y hembra*
> *testigos los testículos solares*
> *falo el pensar y vulva la palabra*
> *espacio es cuerpo signo pensamiento*
> (*L.E.* 162)

Images become at once more direct and more transcendental to express the prophetic plane lying behind the physical:

> los labios negros de la profetisa *Adivinanza*
> (*L.E.* 162)

And in the metaphysical 'instante', thought and mind, body and world become one:

> tu cuerpo son los cuerpos del instante *es cuerpo el tiempo*
> *el mundo*
> visto tocado desvanecido *pensamiento sin cuerpo el cuerpo*
> *imaginario*
> (*L.E.* 163)

The *crescendo* of this passage dies away in a reflective summation of the undifferentiated moment:

> Contemplada por mis óidos   *Horizonte de música tendida*
> olida por mis ojos   *Puente colgante del color al*
> *aroma*
> (*L.E.* 163)

It ends with the revelation that the transcending of the body through union, this passing through the physical realm to one beyond, by denying the finite reality of the corporeal, gives an anchor by which our gaze may meet true reality. Through the form to the idea, but by way of the most intense bodily and spiritual awareness:

> La irrealidad de lo mirado
> Da realidad a la mirada
> (*L.E.* 163)

The final single section leads the poet to the same revelation, but through his nightmare web of word and paradox. Motifs from all earlier sections reappear as he explores the void between appearance and reality, and between affirmation and denial:

> No
> Es una palabra
>   Sí
> Es una palabra
>   Aire son nada
> Son
>   (*L.E.* 164)

Images at first are of agitated movement—'el remolino de las desapariciones . . . El torbellino de las apariciones'—also of the elusiveness of words ('Revoloteando entre las líneas'), and even more of thoughts:

> El pensamiento
>   Revoloteando
> Entre estas palabras.
>   (*L.E.* 165)

But there is constancy too: the footsteps of the woman in the next room, and the birds that come back in the spring, the nim tree which protects against thunder, lightning, and drought.

Opposites combine—black and white in a nocturnal spring, no and yes together, 'Dos sílabas enamoradas'. Physical and conceptual realities deny but complement each other, silence gains meaning only through language:

> El habla
> Irreal
> Da realidad al silencio
>   (*L.E.* 167)

In a subtle play on words reminiscent of the opening lines, silence becomes seal becomes sparkle ('Silencio / Sello / Centelleo') as assonance and consonance reveal again the analogies hidden

behind name and sense. By means of contrast we gain cognizance
of what surrounds us:

> Apariciones y desapariciones
> La realidad y sus resurrecciones
> El silencio reposa en el habla
> (*L.E.* 167)

The poet leads us in a gigantic epistemological circle, at the centre
of which lies 'la transparencia' of which alone he can be sure:

> El espíritu
> Es una invención del cuerpo
> El cuerpo
> Es una invención del mundo
> El mundo
> Es una invención del espíritu
> (*L.E.* 168)

And the final recapitulation juxtaposes the motifs of the moment
of passion, which is also that of mystical insight: her footsteps in
the next room, green thunder, her body naked: 'Como una
sílaba / Como una llama'. Outer reality becomes again 'Haz de
tus imágenes', her body flowing into his, 'Visto / Desvanecido /
Da realidad a la mirada'. Again the transcendence of the physical
in the metaphysical is the Ariadne's thread of the poet in his psychic
labyrinth.

In mythological terms this liberation through passion and
poetry, this reaching of the 'presencia' or 'transparencia' clearly
belongs to the life–death–rebirth pattern basic not only to
religious but to creative thought as well. Mallarmé, for example,
thought of his own poetic gift in precisely these terms, and Mallarmé provides the second epigraph for 'Blanco': 'Avec ce seul
objet dont le Néant s'honore'. The myth of return to a new and
purified life after death formalizes all the cyclic rhythms which
make up our physical as well as our spiritual life: the dawn of each
new day, the return of spring, the sexual release, and in the case
of Paz the emergence of a poem after tortured struggling in the
dark of unformed language. This is akin to the way of the great
mystics in whose writings the death–rebirth myth is given its most
transcendent form. The modern poet's struggle is a secularized
one, but on its own plane the stages of the myth are recognizable
and pertinent. So when Paz, in 'Blanco', reaches consciousness of

himself and his surroundings, and finds himself in the 'dark night' of existential solitude, break-through is doubly possible: in the union of love (Eros, not *caritas*), and in the creation of the poem.

Given the fundamental nature of the myth, one would expect the imagery in which these parallel processes are described to draw heavily on the reflection of the same pattern in Nature, and in fact 'Blanco' contains much chthonic imagery. In 'Blanco' man and poet both pass through the mythical stages, and Nature becomes an objective correlative for both.

The entire poem is an interweaving of the three manifestations of the myth. The opening lines speak of the latent power of the seed which, like the word, must struggle to emerge from a state in which it is 'impar / grávida / nula'. Green is the colour associated with vegetative energy on the chthonic level, and the sunflower with all its evocations of life pushes up towards a 'follaje de claridad'. The rusty gold of the flower speaks to us of the sun, source of cosmic light and heat, and the transition to the fire of passion is made, fire which purifies and renews:

> Pan Grial Ascua
> Muchacha
> (*L.E.* 150)

The dried-up river in the next single section becomes the symbol for the poet's struggles through language to expression:

> El lenguaje
> Es una expiación,
> Propiciación
> Al que no habla . . .
> (*L.E.* 152)

But the section ends with the image of water giving back fertility to arid land and, symbolically, the poem to the anguished poet. The fertility of love also is couched in water imagery in the double section which follows: '*el río los cuerpos | astros infusorios reptiles*', and the river becomes as well '*el río seminal de los mundos*'.

Imagery binds the poet and landscape in a shared agony as the next single section opens (p. 155) on a burning desert:

> Paramera abrasada
> Del amarillo al encarnado
> La tierra es un lenguaje calcinado.
> (*L.E.* 155)

The sun is relentless and unjust, Nature hostile—'En un muro rosado / Tres buitres ahítos'—and the surroundings more surrealistic and more threatening as the earth and the poet suffer throes almost as of birth-pangs to break out of the nightmare:

> Dispersión de cuervos.
> Inminencia de violencias violetas.
> Se levantan los arenales,
> La cerrazón de reses de ceniza.
> (*L.E.* 156)

When salvation is gained it is expressed in chthonic images of regeneration, most significantly the multivalent symbol of the last line:

> Tu cuerpo chorrea cielo
> Tremor
> Tu panza tiembla
> Tus semillas estallan
> Verdea la palabra
> (*L.E.* 157)

Throughout the rest of the poem the same mythic cycle prevails. In the last single section the struggles of the poet with language and with the epistemological paradox leave less room for Nature imagery, but it is still there, in the symbol of the nim tree whose branches silence the thunder and put out the lightning and where 'En su follaje bebe agua la sequía . . .' Significantly, echoing the synthesis which has been reached in the rebirth (the 'transparencia'), thunder has become green, thus also productive and full of promise, at the end of the section:

> Tus pasos en el cuarto vecino
> El trueno verde
> Madura
> En el follaje del cielo
> (*L.E.* 168)

Indeed the multivalency of the image 'el follaje del cielo' may be seen as expressing the final stage of the myth in all the manifestations which have concerned Paz in this poem: natural, passionate, and creative.

But the pattern of myth is also that of religious thought. and the poem's imagery and symbolism return us full circle to the Tantric tradition which its initial visual effect so obviously suggests and which has been touched on earlier in connection with 'Maithuna'. Tantra, both Buddhist and Hindu, is a rite of passage from differentiation to unity, ultimately symbolized in the blending of male and female in sexual union. In this act culminates a carefully prescribed ritual based on the five M's, the five forbidden things (forbidden in orthodox circles, that is): *madya* (liquor), *mamsa* (meat), *matsya* (fish), *mudra* (parched grain or kidney bean), and *maithuna* (sexual intercourse).[12] Tantric rites sanctify all human activity, symbolized in these supposedly unclean ingredients, and the state of enstasy[13] is sought by the ordered and rigorous ceremony which ends with sacramental copulation. The latter is essentially an attempt to return to the original androgyne, the complete creation beyond or before separateness. The human body is seen as a representation of the universe, governed by the same laws of union and separation which produce the constant flux of the physical substances. The exploration of the body represents the pilgrimage through the universe to the holy places of the Tantric rites, and these holy places are objectified in the equally holy parts of the human body.[14] This mystic geography recalls to us and deepens the significance of the chthonic imagery of 'Blanco's' left-hand column with its four stages on the journey of erotic union. Furthermore, the first moment explores passion in terms of fire, this being the sacred element in Hindu Tantra whose rites revived one of the most ancient Indian rituals—sacrifice to the holy flame. In the sanctified union of male and female the Hindu Tantric abandons his sperm as ritual sacrifice to the cosmic fire. Paz draws upon this associative meaning in a line such as 'Pan Grial Ascua' in 'Blanco'. The second of the four moments transforms the woman's body with a water metaphor, 'los ríos de tu cuerpo', which among a myriad other associations recalls the lines from the Tantric poet Sahara who discovers in his own body the holiness of the sacred rivers:

> Here is the sacred Yamuna and here the River Ganges,
> Here are Prayaga and Banaras, here are Sun and Moon.
> Here I have visited in my wanderings shrines and such
>   places of pilgrimage.
> For I have not seen another shrine blissful like my
>   own body.[15]

The exploration of the body is in these terms an act of devotion, a sacramental homage to hidden cosmic mysteries.

Tantric ritual echoes in other images, too. For instance, there is a moment in the central column when the earth becomes a representation of the human body, so that the word is born to the poet as the seed bursts in new life: 'Tus semillas estallan / Verdea la palabra" (*L.E.* 157). But in terms of the metaphor 'semilla' is also semen, and the bursting of the seed is that culminating moment in Buddhist Tantra when the semen which is retained, not shed, climbs the spinal column to burst in the brain and produce the illuminated moment, 'bodhicitta', 'mind of enlightenment'. Then, through the sexual alchemy of the holy rite rigidly observed, the devotee knows freedom from the misery of attachment, that is mystic union. 'Blanco' is not a Tantric text, nor is Paz's transcendence that of the Tantric yogi. Yet he constantly seeks transcendence within his own terms, and of these, the aesthetic and erotic may provide matter for literary criticism.[16] The rebirth which is the climax of 'Blanco' is achieved both through the moment of sexual love and through the emergence of the poem as answer to, and as testimony of, the eternity of time and space. Tantric thought and Tantric art have helped to define the particular, richly associative nature of this testimony.

A logical end to this chapter on Paz's mature poetry and his use of paradox is provided by two of his most recent experiments, *Topoemas* and *Discos visuales*, both published in Mexico in 1968. In these works Paz has proceeded further and very logically in directions which have long preoccupied him. The obvious treatment of 'Blanco' as a spatial and a temporal creation, as I have mentioned earlier, reflects the urge behind these shorter pieces. In them the emphasis is on their spatial impact, that is the poet is making use of one of the prerogatives of the painter. Initially both the *Discos* and the *Topoemas* strike the eye as a meaningful arrangement of signs upon a page, complete in itself. Paz's commentary on the *Topoemas* makes his purpose clear—a 'topoema' combines the elements of *topos* and *poem*. It is a "recurso contra el discurso', spatial poetry as opposed to discursive, temporal poetry. The same holds true for the *Discos*.

From this point they require separate discussion, however, for the *Discos* exist in space, yet also have a temporal dimension; and at the same time a dynamism of physical movement is required to bring them to life. The reader must share in the process of creation, for without his direct intervention there is no poem. It is this participation which, according to Paz, distinguishes these visual discs 'de experiencias artísticas afines, como el poema-objeto surrealista y las obras de la poesía concreta' (*Discos*, inside cover). The unfolding of the page in 'Blanco' and the anti-horizontal reading possibilities which it presents are paralleled here by the slow revolving of the second cardboard circle so that a new fragment of text will appear in the window of the upper cardboard circle. Furthermore, the upper disc is illustrated in significant colours and shapes into which the windows are cut so as to harmonize meaning with visual form. The jacket note calls the *Discos* 'Juego y ceremonia o ceremonia que a la vez es un juego', and it emphasizes the complementary effects of word, colour, and form upon the reader's receptive apparatus. One is tempted to see in Paz's use of the circular form and the spatial return of the poem to its beginnings a parallel with mythic yearnings for the great return and with his own conception of a new era of cyclical time beginning in these our days. But in the present context these are digressions. The immediate point to be made is that an instant effect is produced in the reader by allowing elements of shape and colour to reinforce the no longer horizontal arrangement of words. That is, the linear limitations of the written word are surpassed by harnessing pictorial to conceptual effects.

In the case of the *Topoemas* the process is similar, though less decorative and more metaphysical. The book may aptly be compared with the Renaissance emblem-books as well as with concrete poetry, for there are clear analogies with both. It goes one step beyond paradox in that the necessarily linear presentation of a paradox or of an oxymoronic image is replaced by an immediate visual perception of the concept embodied in the 'topoema'. That is the "recurso contra el discurso". Yet once the eye has grasped the composition of the topoem, if one may translate this coinage, its appeal to the mind causes the reader to play with the concepts expressed therein and their ramifications. Thus like concrete poetry the pattern of words on the page constructs a design which is meaningful in relation to the words themselves; like the emblem-books the emphasis lies less on the decorative than on the underlying seriousness of ideas, often extremely subtle and in almost all the topoems metaphysical in import.

Topoemas provides a climax to the experiences lying behind some of the most elevated poems of *Ladera Este*, 'Sunyata', for instance, or 'Lectura de John Cage', or 'Lo idéntico'. Paradox is still the only human approximation to the metaphysical insights behind these poems, but in the *Topoemas*, by reason of their form, the paradox is able to reach the reader's intuition already fused into synthesis. This is so because there exists just that infinitesimal yet immeasurably great distance between the linear presentation on a conventionally printed page and the immediate perception of 'Nagarjuna', for example. Again it is helpful to return to the distinction drawn by C. S. Lewis (already used in the Introduction to this study) between the poem as *logos* (that which means) and as *poiema* (that which is). For whereas the *Discos visuales* allow the object of art to take precedence over the poem as word (*logos*), the topoem, as Paz conceives it, beautifully balances these symbiotic components as does concrete poetry at its best.

There are six topoems, each explained by a note which clarifies them as, among other things, tributes to a series of new and old poets: 'a José Juan Tablada; a Matsuo Basho . . . a los poetas y calígrafos chinos . . . a Apollinaire, Arp y cummings; y a Haroldo de Campos y el grupo de jóvenes poetas brasileños de *Noigandres* e *Invenção*" (*Topoemas*, Comentario III). Thus the tendency towards a marriage of the conceptual and the visual is already clear. The first, 'Palma del viajero', is nearer to a calligram than a topoem, as the words are arranged on the page to present visually the tree of the title. 'Parábola del movimiento' is similar in conception to the *Discos*, that is, it is itself a paradox, 'fijeza en movimiento', words whose essence is movement, fixed on the page yet with the motor impulse potential within them. (The *Discos* realize this potential in actual fact.) Paz cunningly compares this topoem with chapter 56 of *Rayuela*[17], which of course reinforces the idea of movement inherent in the printed word with all the contradictions which this implies.

The second topoem is called after Nagarjuna, the second-century sage largely responsible for the formulation of Mahayana Buddhism. It embodies visually the concept of *sunyata*—the word 'Niego' descends the page vertically over a division of itself into its parts, 'Ni ego'—and thus the negation of *samsara* which implies a negating ego is itself negated. This process reflects one of the basic problems of all mysticism: how far can the psyche which is aware of a transcendent experience be said to have enjoyed this experience, which by definition is beyond consciousness? In Hindu and Buddhist terms the mind which knows negation must itself be negated in order to merge with the universal mind which is *sunyata*, the void. This process is known as 'prasanga', according to Paz's commentary 'el arte de extraer la "consecuencia necesaria" de nuestras imprudentes afirmaciones y negaciones'. The result is not nothingness, for this is itself a negation of being, but the suspension in a greater whole, whatever the terminology used to name it. (The concision and immediacy of the topoem should be more striking now that a paragraph has been needed to summarize an intuition communicated by Paz in three words.)

The third topoem, 'Ideograma de libertad', simple in appearance, is extraordinarily complex in implication. The word 'sino' is broken into the paradox of its halves, 'sí' and 'no', with the voluntary acts of affirmation and negation which they imply. Paz plays also upon the derivation of 'sino' as a 'duplicado semiculto de *signo*' from *signum*, and meaning a heavenly sign, or constellation. Thus figuratively the topoem is a 'constelación semántica' in true concrete style, but its literal meaning also reinforces and plays upon the figurative.

'Monumento reversible' is in pyramid form extending in either direction from the centre of the page. The natural elements, air, fire, etc., form the rising steps of each pyramid, but when the page is reversed, the sign 'monumento reversible' is replaced by 'Al tiempo irreversible' with the consequent ironic effect on the reader. The last topoem, 'Cifra', returns to the concept of *sunyata* by playing upon the etymology of 'cifra' from the Arab 'sifr' (zero, emptiness) which is apparently 'the Sanskrit word "sunya" derived from the root "svi", "to swell" '.[18] 'Cifra' together with its etymological relative 'cero' therefore forms the diameter of a circle (a zero) whose other radii are the words 'como', repeated four times, and 'Colmo Calma' at right angles to 'Cifra Cero'. Thus the cipher leading to zero, the void, or the absolute, is the union of opposites. Paz says that 'Colmo Calma' may be replaced by any other pair of words of similar length, as long as they start with *c* and 'entablen entre ellas una relación análoga a la del texto'. The formula he describes as 'Cifra (vacío-lleno)→Calma'.

The *Topoemas* may thus be seen as the last step to date in a process which has taken Paz from the simple dialectic (especially

of love) of his early poems, through the harnessing of the subconscious to the conscious mind in surrealism, into the metaphysical
expressions of his last works where paradox plays so large a part.
These topoems might be called the visual resolution of the
mode of paradox. Furthermore, in both 'Blanco' and *Topoemas*
Paz has developed his preoccupation with poetry as an art whose
temporal flow can also be fixed spatially by one means or another—
movement halted and frozen, yet still movement. 'Blanco', for
instance, moves 'de lo en blanco a lo blanco — al blanco', where
it is held before our view both physically and conceptually.
Topoemas makes an initial static impression through the eye, but
the reasoning powers of the viewer then must absorb it through
the discursiveness of the intellect. It remains to be seen if the
poet can move further along these paths of exploration both of the
nature of things and of art itself.

CONCLUSION

THE musical analogy upon which this study is based thus offers help in the construction of a language with which to approach the literary work, in this case a poet's total production. Literature itself is a language, that is a system of signs, whose being rests not in its message but in its system.[1] Criticism therefore is justified not in attempting to elucidate a message, but in clarifying this system, and in constructing for itself a 'meta-language' as a tool, to use Roland Barthes's term. The metaphoric use of modes is such a meta-language, and the analogy which it provides is useful only in so far as it serves this interpretive role. It does not imply, therefore, any loose transference of criteria or terminology from one art-form to another. It merely provides a set of paradigms whose interrelationship establishes a formal background against which to measure and compare other forms and paradigms. This method is particularly apt for the deciphering of Paz's linguistic system, since the core of this system remains so constant within the changing tensions of the language itself. It is therefore offered not as one generally prescribed, but as a tool which has here provided a means to a desired end.

There is another analogy with music which presents itself specifically in relation to the theme of the expanded consciousness, be it in spiritual or aesthetic terms (or both), which is at the heart of Paz's work. It would take a music critic to elaborate this suitably, but in layman's language—yet another linguistic system by which to approach an art-form—the pattern laid down by sonata form, for instance, implies the basic cycle of life, death, and rebirth. At its barest this form is described as exposition, development, and recapitulation, a simple structure to carry many of the most transcendental experiences of Western music. The crux, of course, is the transformation of the theme through the development and the greater depth which it thereby gains before its re-emergence. It is not a repetition, just as the close of 'Piedra de sol' is not a repetition of its opening, though the lines are identical. The work of art, be it music or literature, never forms a closed circle, just as it never provides a final answer. It moves spiral-like to a state of suspension, never wholly inscrutable, never wholly clear, putting, as Barthes says, ' "du sens" dans le monde, mais non pas "un sens" '.[2] The reason why art survives, why Shakespeare and Cervantes still command the attention they do, is precisely because their works are language systems in which the reader intuits an infinite variety of possible meanings, but which never present him with the dogmatism of *a* meaning.

The establishment of a system of modes as a critical tool has meant emphasizing a synchronic, not a diachronic, structure. That is to say that chronology has not been a prime factor in organizing this discussion of Paz's poetry. The modes are chosen to cut across the poetry from the different focuses on which they are based, and are not set up according to the passage of years. Time is certainly a dimension, but it has only as much importance as do other principles such as vocabulary, imagery, and theme. Nevertheless, when one finally stands away from the three volumes, *Libertad bajo palabra*, *Salamandra*, and *Ladera Este*, an over-all analogy with the mythic cycle of transcendence presents itself.

The consciousness of the poet, always sensitive to the demands of his art and aware of his responsibilities to his medium, undergoes many changes in the years which separate youth and maturity. Even when the young poet was railing at the injustices of the human race in 'Entre la piedra y el flor', there was a confidence in him that the dualism of good and evil existed in precisely these terms. The early love poems like 'Bajo tu clara sombra' are full of an exuberance which delights by its buoyancy and its acceptance of joy. *Libertad bajo palabra* works its way through growing moods of solitary anguish to the hard-won insights of the poems of the 40s and 50s, especially ¿*Aguila o sol?*, which shows such tortured awareness of the task of the creator, and *La estación violenta*. Here, as in 'Piedra de sol', a confidence in human solidarity alternates with the frustrated disillusionment in man's ability to find 'otherness' in love or in spiritual kinship. The desire to move beyond the limitations of the human condition and the awareness of growth through pain characterize these years.

Salamandra plunges the hero, as it were, into an underworld of even bleaker travail, and marks the point of greatest struggle both with the implacability of language and with the walls of consciousness which it costs so much to break through. Yet we are never without a glimmer of light, for the same is true of the poem as

Camus said of the novel: 'Even if the novel describes only nostalgia, despair, frustration, it still creates a form of salvation. To talk of despair is to conquer it. Despairing literature is a contradiction in terms.'[3]

Ladera Este affirms this conquest of despair not only in aesthetic but in human terms. The easy dialectic of the early poems has been replaced by a suspension of open condemnation where the political realm is allowed to spill into the poetic. Eroticism has grown in power and urgency because it is now combined with a spiritual kinship so highly valued after years of existential solitude. The metaphysical dimension of the poetry and of Paz's view of poetry itself has deepened by contact with the religious philosophies of the East. These have helped the poet to affirm his beliefs and his humanity, and the form of expression taken by the Sutras and koans has increased Paz's own propensity towards paradox as a stylistic representation of the union of opposites.

Ladera Este would stand in relation to the earlier volumes as the moment of reconciliation which follows early consciousness and developing anguish. Its maturing through suffering is akin to the rebirth stage of the mythic progress of the hero, or to the Jungian individuation which is preceded by a painful recognition of both the light and the dark sides of the psyche. To return to the symphonic analogy, it is the expanded return of earlier motifs in a recapitulation which is not a repetition but a transformation.

The critical method used in order to attempt a synthetic exegesis of Paz's poetry must necessarily appear ungainly in the light of the poetry itself. It is offered in the hope of fulfilling the task of intermediary, which on the creative level is the role of the poet himself. Jung's view of the artist is that he is despite himself the vessel through which 'art realizes its purposes', and that he is forced by the peculiar nature of his experiences to penetrate to the moment when the 'common rhythm' of human existence is reached. This he must then communicate to those who cannot feel it for themselves.[4] Thomas Merton's view reinforces this from the standpoint of the poet himself. He believed that things 'connect up' and that poetry contains clues to connections made but not yet seen.[5] In a very humble way criticism can aim for a similar goal, perhaps leading the reader to some of the connections which the poet with his special vision is trying to make him perceive.

NOTES

INTRODUCTION

1. See Octavio Paz, *Marcel Duchamp o el Castillo de la Pureza* (Mexico, 1968) and *Tamayo en la pintura mexicana* (Mexico, 1959).

2. For more detailed information see Curt Sachs, *The Rise of Music in the Ancient World* (New York, 1943), p. 248 and *passim*, and Gustave Reese, *Music in the Middle Ages* (New York, 1940), p. 10.

3. Amado Alonso, 'La interpretación estilística de los textos literarios', *Materia y forma en poesía* (Madrid, 1955), p. 110.

4. Thomas Merton, *Zen and the Birds of Appetite* (New York, 1968), pp. 71–8.

5. See Alan W. Watts, *The Spirit of Zen* (New York, 1960), p. 49.

6. Quoted by Thomas Merton, *Zen and the Birds of Appetite*, p. 75.

7. Ibid.

8. C. S. Lewis, *An Experiment in Criticism* (Cambridge, 1965), p. 130 and *passim*.

CHAPTER I

1. See Mircea Eliade, *Rites and Symbols of Initiation* (New York, 1965).

2. See id., *Myths, Dreams and Mysteries* (New York, 1967), and also Paz's own discussion of the ideas of Claude Lévi-Strauss in *Claude Lévi-Strauss o el nuevo festín de Esopo* (Mexico, 1969).

3. The relevance of Mexico to Paz has been well discussed by Judith Bernard in her unpublished doctoral dissertation, 'Mexico as Theme, Image and Contribution to Myth in the Poetry of Octavio Paz' (University of Wisconsin, 1964). Hereafter referred to as Bernard.

4. Carlos Fuentes, 'La situación del escritor en América Latina', dialogue with Emir Rodríguez Monegal in *Mundo Nuevo*, i (julio 1966), 5–22.

5. Octavio Paz, *Libertad bajo palabra* (2nd ed., Mexico, 1968); from here on referred to as *Lib.*, and *Ladera Este* (Mexico, 1969), referred to henceforth as *L.E.*

6. Cf. Artemio Cruz in his later years in Carlos Fuentes, *La muerte de Artemio Cruz* (Mexico, 1965).

7. Thus from a socio-political occasion Paz reaches a conclusion identical with the following from twelve years later: '. . . nos sentimos no como un yo aislado ni como un nosotros extraviado en el laberinto de los siglos

sino como una parte del todo, una palpitación en la respiración universal
. . .', Octavio Paz, *Claude Lévi-Strauss o el nuevo festín de Esopo*, p. 125.

8. Octavio Paz, *Salamandra* (Mexico, 1962, 2nd ed., 1969), hereafter referred to as *Sal.*

9. Laurette Séjourné, *Burning Water* (New York, *c.* 1956), p. 77. Hereafter referred to as Séjourné.

10. See discussion of this poem on p. 80 below.

11. Bernard, p. 166.

12. Séjourné, p. 90.

13. C. G. Jung, *Two Essays on Analytical Psychology* (Cleveland and New York, 1965), pp, 200–1.

14. Bernard (p. 182) comes to the conclusion that the 'falda de maíz' may recall the pre-Columbian goddess Coatlicue, whose skirt was formed of intertwined snakes, but that skirts of corn and water are not part of the 'Aztec pantheon' and are used by Paz in a personal symbolism. Erich Neumann in *The Great Mother* (New York, 1955), pp. 177–82, gives an interesting account of Chicomecoatl, the Terrible Mother or Corn Mother, goddess of the seven snakes who was also the goddess of renewal of vegetation through the sex act. She demanded the sacrifice of female victims, sometimes crying for human hearts, or for human blood to drink. She provides a striking parallel with Kali, Hindu goddess of creation through destruction.

15. See Wallace Fowlie, *Age of Surrealism* (New York, 1950), p. 181, as quoted by Bernard, p. 178.

16. See Alfonso Caso, *El Pueblo del Sol* (Mexico, 1953), p. 37, and Séjourné, p. 57, as quoted by Bernard, pp. 162, 163.

17. See Octavio Paz, *Claude Lévi-Strauss*, pp. 20–4.

18. See Edith Hamilton, *Mythology* (New York, 1957), pp. 31–2, quoted by Bernard, p. 176.

19. Octavio Paz, 'Los signos en rotación', *El arco y la lira* (2nd ed., Mexico, 1967), pp. 271–2.

20. Serge Gavronsky, ed., *Poems and Texts* (New York, 1969), p. 2.

21. Ibid., pp. 42–51. It is interesting that here occurs the line: 'Écrit le xxii juin de ma cinquante et unième année: jour du solstice d'été . . .' (italicized in text).

22. Charles Olson, 'Projective Verse', in *Human Universe* (New York, 1967), pp. 51–61.

23. Ibid., p. 55. Paz himself mentions Olson's theories in his essay 'Los nuevos acólitos'', in *Corriente alterna* (Mexico, 1968), pp. 36–9.

24. Nicanor Parra, 'Advertencia al lector', *Poemas y Antipoemas* (3rd ed., Santiago, 1967), p. 72.

25. See *Libertad bajo palabra*, p. 147 and *passim*.

26. See Mircea Eliade, *Myths, Dreams and Mysteries*, pp. 155–90, on 'Mother Earth and the Cosmic Hierogamies'.

27. See discussion of Kali on pp. 32–3 below.

28. See Mircea Eliade, *The Myth of the Eternal Return* (London, 1955).

29. 'El poema ¿no es ese espacio vibrante sobre el cual se proyecta un puñado de signos como un ideograma que fuese un surtidor de significaciones?' (Octavio Paz, 'Los signos en rotación', *El arco y la lira*, p. 270).

30. Octavio Paz, *Ladera Este*, p. 173.

31. The following account of Indian myths is drawn from Heinrich Zimmer, *Myths and Symbols in Indian Art and Civilization* (New York, 1946), and *Philosophies of India* (New York, 1951) by the same author. These are hereafter referred to in the notes as *Myths* and *Philosophies*.

32. Zimmer, *Myths*, p. 215.

33. This explanation of the myth is again drawn from Zimmer, *Myths* and *Philosophies*.

34. The coinciding of the lotus goddess with Prajna-Paramita in Mahayana Buddhism is not pertinent to this group of poems, but will be discussed later in connection with 'Cuento de dos jardines'. See Zimmer's discussion of the lotus goddess in *Myths*, p. 96.

35. Séjourné, p. 137.

36. Zimmer, *Myths*, p. 51.

37. See p. 129 below.

38. Zimmer, *Myths*, p. 197.

39. Ibid., p. 199.

40. Ibid.

41. See Heinrich Zimmer, *The Art of Indian Asia* (New York, 1955), vol. i, 297–8, for a verbal description, and vol. ii, plates 248–65, for photographs. Paz in his note (*L.E.* 181) dates the sculptures as seventh century, Zimmer as eighth.

42. According to Paz, *L.E.* 181. Zimmer does not refer to this desecration.

43. Zimmer, *The Art of Indian Asia*, p. 298.

44. See discussion, p. 149 below, of Paz's concrete poem 'Nagarjuna' in *Topoemas* (Mexico, 1968). My exposition of these doctrines is based on Zimmer, *Philosophies*, pp. 507–34.

45. From the *Madhyamika Sastra*, quoted by Zimmer, *Philosophies*, p. 521

46. Zimmer, *Philosophies*, p. 523.

47. Ibid., p. 524. The *Samyutta-Nikaya* is one of the holy texts of Buddhism.

48. Charles Olson, 'Projective Verse', in *Human Universe*, p. 52.

49. See Zimmer, *Philosophies*, pp. 560–602.

50. Zimmer, *Philosophies*, p. 556.

51. Ibid., p. 555.

52. See discussion on pp. 147–8 below.

53. John Cage, *Silence* (Middletown, Conn., 1961), p. 46.

54. Ibid., p. 34. Cage quotes a conversation between himself and Schoenberg during a lesson. The remark must therefore be taken on trust.

55. John Cage, *A Year from Monday* (Middletown, Conn., 1967), inside cover.

56. Id., *Silence*, p. 8.

57. Ibid., p. 145, as quoted from Meister Eckhart's sermon, 'God made the poor for the rich'.

58. Zimmer, *Myths*, p. 79 and *passim*.

59. Zimmer, *Philosophies*, p. 483 and *passim*.

60. See Chapter III below.

61. In an interesting note (*L.E.* 178) Paz draws this comparison: 'Krishna es azul y negro, como Mixcoatl.' Mixcoatl is described thus in Ignacio Bernal's *Mexico before Cortez* (New York, 1963), p. 129:

'MIXCOATL   Meesh-*coh*-ahtl. Chieftain of the Toltecs at the time of their arrival in the Valley of Mexico in a barbarian state (*ca.* A.D. 900). Father of Topiltzin, founder of Tula and the great culture hero. Mixcoatl was deified by Topiltzin and worshipped as a god from then on.'

It is not the information but the parallel drawn which is pertinent here.

62. See Mircea Eliade, *The Myth of the Eternal Return* (London, 1955) and his *Myths, Dreams and Mysteries*, pp. 47–56.

63. Id., *Myths, Dreams and Mysteries*, p. 23 and *passim*.

64. See also 'La Higuera', in *Libertad bajo palabra*, p. 195.

65. Zimmer, *Myths*, pp. 98–9.

66. See Claude Lévi-Strauss, *Structural Anthropology* (New York, 1963), p. 211. Equally pertinent is the whole of the essay 'The Structural Study of Myth' in that volume.

CHAPTER II

1. See, for instance, Octavio Paz's essay, 'André Bretón o la búsqueda del comienzo', in *Corriente alterna* (Mexico, 1968), pp. 52–64.

2. Reprinted in Guillaume Apollinaire, *Chronique d'art* (Paris, 1960), pp. 426–7. Apollinaire describes the event as a 'point de départ d'une série de manifestations de cet Esprit Nouveau, qui . . . ne manquera pas de seduire l'élite et se promet de modifier de fond en comble les arts et les mœurs dans l'allégresse universelle . . .' (p. 426).

Paz's title *La estación violenta* is in fact a translation of a line from Apollinaire's 'La Jolie Rousse'—'Voici que vient l'été la saison violente'— and he prefaces the volume with another line from the same poem: 'O Soleil c'est le temps de la Raison ardente.'

3. André Breton, 'Manifeste du Surréalisme' (1924). Reprinted in *Manifestes du Surréalisme*, ed. Jean-Jacques Pauvert (Paris, 1962), p. 39.

4. Breton, *Manifestes* . . ., p. 27.

5. Ibid., p. 40.

6. Paul Ilie, 'Two More Spanish Surrealists', *Books Abroad*, xliii, 2 (Spring 1969), 189–93.

7. See 'La palabra edificante', Octavio Paz's critical essay on Cernuda in *Cuadrivio* (Mexico, 1959), pp. 165–203.

8. Stéphane Mallarmé, 'Le tombeau d'Edgar Poe', *Poésies* (Paris, 1945), p. 128.

9. Mary Ann Caws, *Surrealism and the Literary Imagination* (The Hague, 1966), p. 54.

10. Jean-Paul Sartre, 'L'art poétique', as quoted by Caws, p. 54, with no further documentation.

11. See Gwendolyn Bays, *The Orphic Vision* (Lincoln, Nebr., 1964).

12. Yves Duplessis, in *Le Surréalisme* (Paris, 1961), p. 90, quotes Robert Desnos: 'Je ne crois pas en Dieu, mais j'ai le sens de l'Infini. Nul n'a l'esprit plus religieux que moi.'

13. I use the term in its Jungian sense. See C. G. Jung, 'Psychological Commentary', in *The Tibetan Book of the Great Liberation*, ed. W. Y. Evans-Wentz (Oxford, 1969), p. xlvi.

14. Isidore Lucien Ducasse, alias Comte de Lautréamont, *Les Chants de Maldoror* (Paris, 1963), p. 182.

15. Cf. the image of Reverdy quoted by Breton, *Manifestes* . . ., p. 52: 'Le monde rentre dans un sac.'

16. C. G. Jung, *Two Essays on Analytical Psychology* (Cleveland and New York, 1965), p. 232.

17. See Mary Ann Caws's discussion of the subject, *Surrealism and the Literary Imagination*, p. 40.

18. Octavio Paz, *Corriente alterna*, p. 56.

19. Id., 'Los signos en rotación', *El arco y la lira* (Mexico, 1967), p. 261.

20. Quoted without source in Yves Duplessis, *Le Surréalisme*, p. 31.

21. See pp. 94–101 for an interpretation of 'noon' in Paz's work.

22. André Breton, *Poèmes* (Paris, 1948), p. 99. Cf. the line 'Qui s'était fait un masque de mes traits', quoted in Mary Ann Caws, *Surrealism* . . ., p. 41.

23. Oscar Wilde, *The Picture of Dorian Gray* (New York, 1931).

CHAPTER III

1. Dámaso Alonso, *Poesía española* (Madrid, 1966), p. 19, quotes from F. de Saussure's *Cours de linguistique générale* (Paris, 1949), p. 128 and *passim*.

2. A term coined by Charles Bally in 'L'arbitraire du signe', *Le Français moderne*, viii (1940), pp. 193–206; pp. 195 f. Quoted in Stephen Ullmann, *Language and Style* (New York, 1964), p. 11. For a discussion of 'name' and 'sense' see Ullmann, p. 18 and *passim*.

3. I exclude 'Blanco' from this discussion, as it will be analysed in the final chapter.

4. One is reminded of another poet's ironical path to this same conclusion. Cf. Nicanor Parra, 'Cambios de nombre', in *Versos de salón* (Santiago, 1962), pp. 7–8:

El poeta no cumple su palabra
Si no cambia los nombres de las cosas.
¿Mis zapatos parecen ataúdes?
Sepan que desde hoy en adelante
Los zapatos se llaman ataúdes.

5. Alfred de Musset, 'La Nuit de mai', *Oxford Book of French Verse* (Oxford, 1951), p. 381.

6. See Roger Caillois, 'Le Complexe de midi', *Minotaure*, no. 9, as quoted by Mary Ann Caws, *Surrealism and the Literary Imagination* (The Hague, 1966), p. 65.

7. The same is true of Wordsworth's daffodils, which the same psychic process holds in the mind for future inspiration:

They flash upon that inward eye
which is the bliss of solitude.

See 'I Wandered Lonely as a Cloud', *Selections from Wordsworth*, ed. Philip Wayne (London, 1932), p. 52.

8. C. G. Jung, *Two Essays on Analytical Psychology* (Cleveland and New York, 1956), p. 38.

9. Cf. Nathalie Sarraute, *Between Life and Death*, trans. María Jolas (New York, 1969).

10. Stephen Ullmann, *Language and Style*, p. 18, uses 'name' and 'sense' to simplify the terminology of C. K. Ogden and I. A. Richards in *The Meaning of Meaning* (London, 1936), p. 11. Ogden and Richards called the 'name' 'symbol', the 'sense' 'thought or reference', and the 'thing' referred to the 'referent'.

11. A very interesting example of the 'sense' which Paz demands of the 'name' *transparencia* occurs in his book, *Claude Lévi-Strauss o el nuevo festín de Esopo* (Mexico, 1969), pp. 117–18, in which Paz compares one aspect of Kant's philosophy with that of Lévi-Strauss: 'Para Kant hay un sujeto y un objeto; Lévi-Strauss borra esa distinción. En lugar del

sujeto postula un 'nosotros' hecho de particularidades que se oponen y combinan. El sujeto se veía a sí mismo y los juicios del entendimiento universal eran los suyos. El 'nosotros' no puede verse: no tiene un sí mismo, su intimidad es exterioridad. Sus juicios no son suyos: es el vehículo de un juicio. Es la extrañeza en persona. Ni siquiera puede saberse una cosa entre las cosas: es una transparencia a través de la cual una cosa, el espíritu, mira a las otras cosas y se deja mirar por ellas. Al abolir el sujeto, Lévi-Strauss destruye el diálogo de la conciencia consigo misma y el diálogo del sujeto con el objeto.'

12. For a discussion of 'the longing for a god . . . deeper, and stronger perhaps than the love for a human person', see C. G. Jung, *Two Essays on Analytical Psychology*, p. 143 and *passim*.

13. See Rudolf Otto, *The Idea of the Holy* (London, 1969), pp. 14–15 and *passim*.

14. C. G. Jung, op. cit., p. 81 and *passim*.

CHAPTER IV

1. See Lucien Lévy-Bruhl, *La Mentalité primitive* (Paris, 1960), p. 17 and *passim*.

2. C. G. Jung, *Two Essays in Analytical Psychology* (Cleveland and New York, 1965), p. 82.

3. See, for instance, Octavio Paz's recent prose work, *Conjunciones y disyunciones* (Mexico, 1969).

4. C. G. Jung, *Mysterium Conjunctionis* (New York, 1963), pp. 501–2.

5. See Rupert Allen, 'An Analysis of Narrative and Symbol in Lorca's "Romance sonámbulo" ', *Hispanic Review*, xxxvi, 4 (Oct. 1969), 338–52.

6. See Jung, *Mysterium Conjunctionis*, p. 240 and *passim*.

7. See ibid., p. 502.

8. Octavio Paz, 'La Pensée en blanc', *Art tantrique* (Paris, 1970), n.p.

9. Author's note (c) following 'Blanco' in all its editions. Other references to the poem will quote pagination from the volume *Ladera Este*.

10. See 'Ideograma de libertad', *Topoemas* (Mexico, 1968), and 'La Pensée en blanc'.

11. See Laurette Séjourné, *Burning Water* (New York, 1956), pp. 99–101.

12. For a full explanation see Agehananda Bharati, *The Tantric Tradition* (London, 1965), p. 242 and *passim*.

13. See definition and use of this term by Mircea Eliade in *Yoga: Immortality and Freedom* (New York, 1958), and in Bharati, op. cit., pp. 285–7.

14. Bharati, op. cit., pp. 84–100.

15. Bharati, op. cit., p. 92. Also quoted by Paz in French translation in 'La Pensée en Blanc'.

16. See Thomas Merton's essay, 'The Transcendent Experience', in his book *Zen and the Birds of Appetite* (New York, 1968).

17. Julio Cortázar, *Rayuela* (Buenos Aires, 1969). This novel is arranged in a circular and therefore unending form, each chapter concluding with the number of the chapter to be read next, jumping back and forth in "hopscotch" form and finally oscillating between chapters 58 and 131. Chapter 56 is especially pertinent to the topoem in question by virtue of its thematic content: perpetually unresolved movement.

18. Edward Conze, *Buddhism*, as quoted by Paz in 'Comentario' to *Topoemas*.

CONCLUSION

1. See Roland Barthes, 'Qu'est-ce que la critique?', in *Essais critiques* (Paris, 1964), pp. 252–7.

2. Ibid., p. 256.

3. Albert Camus, *The Rebel*, trans. Anthony Bower (New York, 1960), p. 263.

4. C. G. Jung, 'Psychology and Literature', *Modern Man in Search of a Soul* (New York, 1969), pp. 152–72.

5. See the interview with John Howard Griffin, 'In Search of Thomas Merton', Magazine Section, *Louisville Courier-Journal* (7 Dec. 1969), p. 54.

SELECT BIBLIOGRAPHY

The most complete bibliography on Octavio Paz to date is that of Alfredo A. Roggiano, 'Bibliografía de y sobre Octavio Paz', *Revista Iberoamericana*, xxxvii, núm. 71 (enero–marzo de 1971), 269–97.

ALLEN, Rupert. 'An Analysis of Narrative and Symbol in Lorca's "Romance sonámbulo"', *Hispanic Review*, xxxvi, 4 (Oct. 1969), 338–52.

ALONSO, Amado. *Materia y forma en poesía*. Madrid, 1955.

ALONSO, Dámaso. *Poesía española*. Madrid, 1966.

APOLLINAIRE, Guillaume. *Chronique d'art*. Paris, 1960.

BALLY, Charles. 'L'arbitraire du signe', *Le Français moderne*, viii (1940) 193–206.

BARTHES, Roland. *Essais critiques*. Paris, 1964.

BASHO, Matsuo. *Sendas de Oku*, trans. O. Paz and E. Hayashiya. 1st ed., Mexico, 1957; 2nd ed., Mexico, 1971.

BAYS, Gwendolyn. *The Orphic Vision*. Lincoln, Nebr., 1964.

BERNAL, Ignacio. *Mexico before Cortez*. New York, 1963.

BERNARD, Judith A. 'Mexico as Theme, Image and Contribution to Myth in the Poetry of Octavio Paz.' Unpubl. doc. diss., University of Wisconsin, 1964.

—— 'Myth and Structure in Octavio Paz's *Piedra de sol*', *Symposium*, xxi, 1 (1967), 5–13.

BHARATI, Agehananda. *The Tantric Tradition*. London, 1965.

BOSQUET, Alain. 'Octavio Paz, ou le séisme pensif', *Nouvelle Revue Française*, 14ᵉ année, no. 168 (Dec. 1966), 1071–5.

BRETON, André. *L'Amour fou*. Paris, 1937.

—— 'Manifeste du Surréalisme' (1924), *Manifestes du Surréalisme*, ed. J.-J. Pauvert. Paris, 1962.

—— *Nadja*. Paris, 1964.

—— *Poèmes*. Paris, 1948.

BURY, John Bagnell. *The Idea of Progress*. New York, 1955.

CAGE, John. *A Year from Monday*. Middletown, Conn., 1967.

—— *Silence*. Middletown, Conn., 1961.

CAMUS, Albert. *The Rebel*, trans. Anthony Bower. New York, 1960.

CASO, Alfonso. *El Pueblo del Sol*. Mexico, 1953.

CAWS, Mary Ann. *Surrealism and the Literary Imagination*. The Hague, 1966.

CÉA, Claire. *Octavio Paz, étude*. Paris, 1965.

COHEN, J. M. *Poesía de nuestro tiempo*. Mexico, 1964.

CONZE, Edward. *Buddhism, its Essence and Development*. Oxford, 1953.

DUCASSE, Isidore Lucien, alias Comte de Lautréamont. *Les Chants de Maldoror*. Paris, 1963.

DUPLESSIS, Yves. *Le Surréalisme*. Paris, 1961.

DURÁN, Manuel. 'Libertad y erotismo en la poesía de Octavio Paz', *Sur*, cclxxvi (1962), 72–7.

DURAND, José. 'Octavio Paz', *Américas*, xv, 8 (1963), 30–3.

ELIADE, Mircea. *Myths, Dreams and Mysteries*. New York, 1967.
—— *Rites and Symbols of Initiation*. New York, 1965.
—— *The Myth of the Eternal Return*. London, 1955.
—— *Yoga: Immortality and Freedom*. New York, 1958.

EMBEITA, María. 'Octavio Paz, poesía y metafísica', *Insula*, xxiii, 260–1 (julio–agosto 1968), 12.

FEIN, John M. 'The Mirror as Image and Theme in the Poetry of Octavio Paz', *Symposium*, x (1956), 251–70.

FOWLIE, Wallace. *Age of Surrealism*. New York. 1950.

FUENTES, Carlos. *La muerte de Artemio Cruz*. Mexico, 1965.
—— 'La situación del escritor en América Latina', *Mundo Nuevo*, i (julio 1966), 5–22.

GAVRONSKY, Serge, ed. *Poems and Texts*. New York, 1969.

HAMILTON, Edith. *Mythology*. New York, 1957.

ILIE, Paul. 'Two More Spanish Surrealists', *Books Abroad*, xliii, 2 (Spring 1969), 189–93.

JOBES, Gertrude. *Dictionary of Mythology, Folklore and Symbols*. 3 vols. New York, 1961.

JUNG, C. J. *Modern Man in Search of a Soul*. New York, 1969.
—— *Mysterium Conjunctionis*. New York, 1963.
—— 'Psychological Commentary', in *The Tibetan Book of the Great Liberation*, ed. W. Y. Evans-Wentz. Oxford, 1969.
—— *Two Essays on Analytical Psychology*. Cleveland and New York, 1965.

KING, Lloyd. 'Surrealism and the Sacred in the Aesthetic of Octavio Paz', *Hispanic Review*, xxxvii, 3 (July 1969), 383–93.

LANE, Michael, ed. *Structuralism: a Reader*. London, 1970.

LARREA, Elba M. 'Octavio Paz, poeta de América', *Revista Nacional de Cultura* (Caracas), xxvi, 162–3 (1964), 78–88.

LEIVA, Raul. *Imagen de la poesía mexicana contemporánea*. Mexico, 1959.

LÉVI-STRAUSS, Claude. *Structural Anthropology*. New York, 1963.

LÉVY-BRUHL, Lucien. *La Mentalité primitive*. Paris, 1960.

LEWIS, C. S. *An Experiment in Criticism*. Cambridge, 1965.

MALLARMÉ, Stéphane. *Poésies*. Paris, 1945.

MERTON, Thomas. *Zen and the Birds of Appetite*. New York, 1968.

MUSSET, Alfred de. 'La Nuit de mai', *Oxford Book of French Verse*. Oxford, 1951.

NEUMANN, Erich. *The Great Mother*. New York, 1955.

NUGENT, Robert. 'Structure and Meaning in Octavio Paz's *Piedra de sol*', *Kentucky Foreign Language Quarterly*, xiii (1966), 138–46.

OGDEN, C. K., and RICHARDS, I. A. *The Meaning of Meaning*. London, 1936.

OLSON, Charles. 'Projective Verse', *Human Universe*. New York. 1967, pp. 51–61.

OTTO, Rudolf. *The Idea of the Holy*. London, 1969.

PANICO, Marie Joan. 'Motifs and Expression in Octavio Paz: an Explication of his Spoken Anthology.' Unpubl. doc. diss., University of Maryland, 1966.

PARRA, Nicanor. *Versos de salón*. Santiago, 1962.

PAZ, Octavio, comp. *Anthology of Mexican Poetry*, trans. Samuel Beckett. Bloomington, Ind., 1958; also London, 1958.

—— *Claude Lévi-Strauss o el nuevo festín de Esopo*. Mexico, 1967.

—— *Conjunciones y disyunciones*. Mexico, 1969.

—— *Corriente alterna*. Mexico, 1968.

—— *Cuadrivio*. Mexico, 1959.

—— *Discos visuales*. Mexico, 1968.

—— 'e. e. cummings', trans. Lysander Kemp. *The New Review*, i (Fall 1967), 6–11.

—— *El arco y la lira*. Mexico, 1967.

—— *El laberinto de la soledad*. Mexico, 1969.

—— *La centena (Poemas: 1935–1968)*. Barcelona, 1969.

—— *Ladera Este*. Mexico, 1969.

—— *Las peras del olmo*. Mexico, 1957.

—— *Libertad bajo palabra*. 1st ed., Mexico, 1960.

—— *Libertad bajo palabra*. 2nd ed., Mexico, 1968.

—— *Marcel Duchamp o el castillo de la pureza*. Mexico, 1969.

—— *Posdata*. Mexico, 1970.

—— *Puertas al campo*. Mexico, 1960.

—— *Salamandra*. 1st ed., Mexico, 1962.

—— *Salamandra*. 2nd ed., Mexico, 1969.

—— *Tamayo en la pintura mexicana*. Mexico, 1959.

—— *Topoemas*. Mexico, 1968.

—— Ali Chumacero, José Emilio Pacheco, and Homero Aridjis, eds. *Poesía en movimiento, México 1915–1966*. Mexico, 1969.

REESE, Gustave. *Music in the Middle Ages*. New York, 1940.

Revista Iberoamericana, núm. 74 (enero–marzo de 1971). Issue devoted to Octavio Paz.

SACHS, Curt. *The Rise of Music in the Ancient World*. New York, 1943.

SÁNCHEZ, José G. 'Aspects of Surrealism in the Work of Octavio Paz.' Unpubl. doc. diss., University of Colorado, 1969.

SARRAUTE, Nathalie. *Between Life and Death*, trans. Maria Jolas. New York, 1969.

SAUSSURE, F. de. *Cours de linguistique générale*. Paris, 1949.

SEGALL, Brenda. 'Symbolism in Octavio Paz's "Puerta Condenada"', *Hispania*, liii, 2 (May 1970), 212–19.

SÉJOURNÉ, Laurette. *Burning Water*. New York, 1956.

SIRGADO, Isabel M. Cid de. 'En torno a *El laberinto de la soledad* de Octavio Paz', *Hispanófila*, xxxvii (Sept. 1969), 59–64.

SOUZA, Raymond D. 'The World Symbol and Synthesis in Octavio Paz', *Hispania*, xlvii, 1 (Mar. 1964), 60–5.

ULLMANN, Stephen. *Language and Style*. New York, 1964.

WATTS, Alan W. *The Spirit of Zen*. New York, 1960.

WILDE, Oscar. *The Picture of Dorian Gray*. New York, 1931.

WING, George G. 'Octavio Paz: Poetry, Politics and the Myth of the Mexican.' Unpubl. doc. diss., University of California, 1961.

XIRAU, Ramón. 'La poesía de Octavio Paz', *Cuadernos Americanos*, x, 4 (julio–agosto 1951), 288–98.

—— 'Nota a Octavio Paz', *Insula*, xvii, 184 (1962), 3.

—— 'Notas a *Piedra de sol*', *Universidad de Mexico*, xii, 6 (1958), 15–16.

—— *Octavio Paz, el sentido de la palabra*. Mexico, 1970.

—— *Poesía hispanoamericana y española*. Mexico, 1961.

—— *Poetas de México y España*. Madrid, 1962.

—— *Tres poetas de la soledad*. Mexico, 1955.

ZIMMER, Heinrich. *Myths and Symbols in Indian Art and Civilization*. New York, 1946.

—— *Philosophies of India*. New York, 1951.

—— *The Art of Indian Asia*. 2 vols. New York, 1955.

INDEX OF POEMS DISCUSSED